The Book of

DUNSTER

The Book of

DUNSTER

HILARY BINDING

HALSGROVE

First published in Great Britain in 2002

This book is dedicated to George and Joseph.
May they grow up to know
and love their heritage.

Frontispiece photograph: *Jim Bond, postman in Dunster from c.1920 to 1950.*

British Library Cataloguing-in-Publication Data
A CIP record for this title is available from the British Library

ISBN 1 84 114 2093

HALSGROVE

Halsgrove House
Lower Moor Way
Tiverton, Devon EX16 6SS
Tel: 01884 243242
Fax: 01884 243325
email: sales@halsgrove.com
website: www.halsgrove.com

Printed and bound in Great Britain by Bookcraft Ltd, Midsomer Norton

FOREWORD

Hilary Binding's renown as a historian coupled with her skill as a writer have produced this fascinating amalgam of facts, stories, personalities and pictures relating to the Town of Dunster – 'Town' by ancient charter granting it the status of a market town.

This book will bring pleasure to all of us who are fortunate enough to have been connected with Dunster for either long or short periods as well as to visitors for whom it will embellish the more prosaic information provided by guide books and potted histories.

The author deserves our wholehearted thanks and congratulations on the results of her painstaking research into the past and present life of Dunster.

WALTER LUTTRELL
AUGUST 2002

Dunster Remembered...

Dunster town standith in a botom. The paroch church is set in ground somewhat rising. There is a very celebrate market at Dunstorre ons a wekes. There is a fair privilegid to be at Dunster every Whitsun Mone-day. The town of Dunnestorre makith cloth. The Moions buildid the right goodly and strong castelle of Dunnestorre.

John Leland, 1538.

A little Markett Towne on a flatt altogether environed with hills except towards ye Sea... Sir John Lutterell, whose faire house built on ye Castell Mount is the greatest ornament of ye Place.

Thomas Gerard, 1633.

I am at last returned from my Somersetshire expedition... I think the country abounds with beautiful prospects... I was mightily pleased with Dunster Castle, near Minehead. It stands upon a great eminence, and hath a prospect of that town, with an extensive view of the Bristol Channel, in which are seen two small islands, the Steep Holmes and the Flat Holmes, and on t'other side we plainly distinguished the divisions of fields on the Welsh coast. All the journey I performed on horseback.

John Gay, 1732.

We passed Dunster on our right, a small town between the brow of a hill and the sea. I remember eyeing it wistfully as it lay below us, contrasted with the woody scene around, it looked as clear, as pure, as embrowned and ideal as any landscape I have seen since...

William Hazlitt, *My First Acquaintance with Poets*, 1823.

The artist J.M.W. Turner visited Dunster in 1820.

Contents

Wesley Gould knew his onions! These fine specimens won first prize at the Horticultural Show in 1990.

INTRODUCTION

Dunster must be the most written about, most pictured and most visited village in West Somerset. It is exceptional in so many ways. Set below the foothills of Exmoor and close to the Bristol Channel, its ancient castle towering over all, its glorious church, evocative buildings and working corn mill all point to the fact that Dunster has been an important small market town for centuries. The castle and mill date from before the Domesday Book and for nearly five hundred years the woollen industry thrived, bringing wealth to the people who enjoyed a weekly market and biennial fair. Skilled craftsmen – silversmiths, embroiderers – settled in the town. The lords of the manor, first the de Mohuns and then the Luttrells, played an important role in local and national affairs and the castle was besieged during the Civil War. The Luttrells particularly, were devoted to the place as exemplified by their collection of archives, well documented by William Prynne in the 1600s and now kept carefully in Somerset Record Office.

After the decline of the woollen industry, the nineteenth century saw the town pick itself up and develop as a commercial centre with shops and craftsmen serving many nearby villages. By then tourists had begun to visit and Dunster adapted in order to provide for them. Fortunately the Luttrell family owned most of the village and held inappropriate development in check so that Dunster remains unspoiled and this, at the start of the twenty-first century, is what is appreciated by visitors though many may not realise the story that lies behind what they see.

When I first became interested in the history of Dunster while working with schoolchildren and further education classes, there were forthright people who said: 'We've had enough of Dunster's history ; we don't need any more.' But I was aware that there were few people who had really read the classic books on Dunster's past and few visitors who ventured beyond the High Street with the Luttrell Arms, Yarn Market, shops and tearooms and castle in the background.

When I first set pen to paper in an attempt to head people further into West Street and to the church, the dovecote and the tithe barn, I didn't venture beyond 1900 realising the pitfalls that lie in wait for people daring to tackle really recent history. But since then I have come to realise that Dunster is a living community and that to ignore the last hundred years is to insult the people whose families have lived here for so many generations.

Kit Baker, Ada Philips, Florrie and Winnie Poole on the grassy triangle at the foot of Dunster Steep, c.1927. Behind them the RAC man directs traffic.

The last century of Dunster's story is all about people. The buildings may reflect its history but it is the people who have carried the town into the present day. During the past century the family at the castle mingled with the craftsmen and shopkeepers who served the community. Dunster's vitality was reflected in the extravagant events laid on to celebrate national occasions, well remembered by those who were children at the time.

This book does not pretend to be a new history – there are many historical questions that still need to be investigated. Nor is it a detailed account of the changes that took place in the twentieth century. Rather it tries to show how ordinary people lived, worked and enjoyed life over the years.

The types of events taking place in the town have changed. Today 'Dunster by Candlelight' takes pride of place while a new clubhouse has recently been built on the football ground. There is a children's playground near Gallox Bridge – fortunately criminals are no longer taken on that route to the gallows – and at the time of writing there are plans for turning the tithe barn into a centre of community use for the town.

I have been lucky enough to be lent many photographs and am particularly grateful to the Lyddon family for those taken by James Date, foremost and earliest of local photographers, in the 1860s and '70s. Identification of old photographs is not always easy. Costume helps when people are involved but even then we have to remember that ordinary people were not in the forefront of fashion; they kept and altered their clothes over years and may have had them handed down in the first place from the gentry.

Views can be even more difficult to date. Sometimes it is impossible to stand in the exact spot where the photographer took the shot. Take for example the view across the village *(see page 45)* to the castle taken before Northanger and Priory Thatch were built.

William Hobbs in Dunster Church. Billy had connections with Dumbledeer and learnt some tailoring in Withycombe before coming to live in Aville. He and his wife, Emma, later lived at Windwhistle near Broadwood before moving into Dunster. He loved music, played the accordion and had an old-fashioned gramophone, with brass-band records – no one was allowed to speak while they played. Billy spent hours in the church and this photograph was taken at the time the church organ was being renovated. He was 'the dearest of men'.

In 1954 most of the village properties were sold, initially to the tenants, when the Luttrell estate had to be broken up. The castle gardens are an exemplar of how people have cared for Dunster since then. In the centre of the town are the Village Gardens, where people can sit quietly and which also provide an area for play and for village concerts. Beside the church is the Memorial Garden, given to Dunster in perpetuity by Geoffrey and Alys Luttrell. On the site of the Melon Garden is a new house with behind it the old castle glasshouses. The dovecote stands at the foot of the once Priory (or Vicarage) Garden; the old Vicarage vegetable garden is (at the time of writing) cared for by a garden-loving rector.

The Book of Dunster is largely compiled from the memories and pictures of Dunster people, past and present. Over the last twenty years many individuals have researched aspects of the social history of the town and ensured the preservation of pictures and documents. Others have recorded special events in words and photographs or written down their memories for posterity.

Many people have contributed to this book and I feel privileged to have been asked to compile it.

ACKNOWLEDGEMENTS

This book is a community effort but as compiler I would like to thank everyone who has contributed in any way.

Particular thanks go to:

Sir Walter Luttrell for his encouragement and for lending me the text of his talk, given at the castle for the National Trust a few years ago, which forms the basis of Chapters Thirteen and Fourteen – thanks also go to him and to Mr Julian Luttrell for lending me family photographs; Carol and Arthur Ell for the loan of very many photographs and for their devotion to the preservation of records of old Dunster; Margaret Gould for all her support and her chivvying, for the loan of many photographs, for information and for help with captions; the Lyddon family for the use of James Date's photographs; Hilda Parham for all her infectious enthusiasm, for the loan of many photographs and for information about shops particularly – her memories form the basis of Chapter Eleven; Peter and Margaret Tudball for all their help, for the loan of photographs and for information – Peter's memories form the basis of Chapter Twelve.

Many other people have contributed to the book. If I have inadvertently left anyone out I do apologise. While I have relied on information given to me, any errors are my own.

Thanks must also go to Steve Bowden for photographs of his mother's family and the Luttrell Arms Garage; Norman Case for photographs; Margaret Chorley for her photograph of William Hobbs; June Copp for information and the delightful photographs of her father; Eleanor Crane for information about the market and the school; Bob Cruxford; Mr F. Clitsome; Bill Dainton for photographs, including some of his wife Olive's family, and useful information; Phyl Fennell; David Jessup for his line drawings made for *Discovering Dunster*; Mrs Joan Jordan; June Land; Karl Meddick for information about carol singing and Mike Dibble for a fine photograph of carol singers; John Melbourne; Bob Nicholson for help with details about the hospital, and Joan for producing some school pictures when I was desperate; Sylvia Parsons; Muriel Petford for information and for photographs of the Dyer family; the late Miss Prior; Somerset Archaeological and Natural History Society; Somerset Record Office for allowing me easy access to Dunster papers; Muriel Roy; Norman Stanley; Mrs Bet Sully; Samantha Twigge; Joan Vaulter for photographs of Aville Farm and of John Vaulter with his vegetable cart; Mr J.J. Webber; Gill White of Leighland and Roberta Woods of Winnipeg for the Vowles album of photographs from Canada; Rob Wilson-North.

HILARY BINDING, 2002.

A pause during the Festival of Britain celebrations, 1951.

Fun & Games

Left: *Winter sports.* Left to right: *Gilbert Sparkes, Eric Yandle, Jack Haydon, Jack Baker, Tom Poole.*

Right: *Where were these solemn young men going? Was it a meeting of the Ancient Order of Foresters?* Back row, last but one: *Arthur Tudball.* Second row, third from left: *J.H. Parham;* sixth from left: *? Tudball;* ninth from left: *Joe Locker.*

Above: *Waiting for hounds, c.1910.*

Florrie and Winnie Poole with (centre) Douglas Dyer's Aunt Jane, c.1927.

Books & References

N.V. Allen, *Churches and Chapels of Exmoor*, Exmoor Press 1974.
Florence Chuk, *The Somerset Years*, Pennard Hill Publications 1987.
Revd J. Collinson, *History of the Antiquities of the County of Somerset*, Crutwell 1791.
Bernard Concannon, *The History of Dunster Beach*, Monkspath Books 1995.
E.M. Crane, *The Village School, Dunster 1861–1945*, Pp. 1981.
J. Dixon and H.P. Williams, *Parish Surveys: Carhampton*, SANHS 1981.
F.C. Eeles, *Guide to St George's Church, Dunster.*
Grahame Farr, *Somerset Harbours*, Johnson 1954.
L.V. Grinsell, *The Archaeology of Exmoor*, David and Charles 1970.
Preb. F. Hancock, *Dunster Church and Priory*, Barnicott and Pearce 1905.
T.A. Kent, 'Edward Sweet: A West Country Silversmith', *Proceedings of the Silver Society*, 1870–72.
L. Lamplugh, *Minehead and Dunster*, Phillimore 1987.
H.C. Maxwell-Lyte, *Dunster and its Lords*, Pp. 1882.
H.C. Maxwell-Lyte, *A History of Dunster*, St Catherine's Press 1887.
G. Metcalf and A.R. Thomas, *Dunster Water Mill.*
R.W. Patten, *Exmoor Custom and Song*, Exmoor Press 1974.
A.G. Pointon, *Methodism in West Somerset 1790–1981*, Pp. 1982.
Hazel Riley and Robert Wilson-North, *The Field Archaeology of Exmoor*, English Heritage 2001.
D.J. Stevens, *War and Peace in West Somerset 1620–1670*, Pp. 1988.
A.J. Trayhurn, *Dunster in 1460*, Cox 1951.

Dunster School, c.1914–16. Fourth row: *Kit Baker* (fifth from left), *Dolly Wedlake* (sixth from left); third row: *Lily Tame* (eighth from left); second row: *Queenie Parham* (first on left), *Joan Hole* (seventh from left); front row: *Jack Parham* (second from left) *and Reg Vaulter* (far right). *Mr Cantle* (left) *was headmaster at the time.*

Bat's Castle

Bat's Castle from the air with the Gallox Hill hill-slope enclosure in the background.
(Cambridge University Collection: copyright reserved.)

Chapter One

Early Years

Fifteen hundred years before Dunster Castle was built, people of the tribe of the Dumnonii were living on the hills above the River Avill in scattered enclosed settlements, growing crops in small fields and keeping tough and wiry sheep, goats and pigs. One of these settlements was the hill-slope enclosure on Gallox Hill, which, with the recently discovered enclosure on Grabbist Hill, overlooked the Avill Valley, perhaps indicating an element of defence in their siting. An extensive later prehistoric field system on Withycombe Common nearby gives us an idea of how the land was cultivated.

Bat's Castle, little more than a slingshot from the Gallox Hill site, is a much more elaborate hill-fort with inner and outer ramparts, a complex eastern entrance and extensive outworks to the south-east and north-west designed to impress and dominate the landscape and maybe to keep people out. Hazel Riley and Robert Wilson-North in *The Field Archaeology of Exmoor* suggest that Bat's Castle was the seat of the élite of society and that it might have been 'a focal point in the landscape, an awe-inspiring and sacred place, designed to be viewed from a distance.' It has also been suggested that besides fulfilling ritual and religious functions it might have been the commercial centre for the community with storage facilities for grain, leather and wool while crafts such as smithing may also have been carried out, as was the case at nearby Timberscombe. Sites in this area were not only close to centres of early iron smelting but had access to the sea and trading links with the people of Iberia and Brittany.

Looking up the Avill Valley in c.1910.

Tradition links the Romans with Bat's Castle – it is often referred to by local people as the Roman Camp – although a hoard of Roman coins discovered by schoolboys playing in the ramparts in 1983 is unlikely to have been deposited in the Roman period. There were eight coins altogether with a large date span from 102BC to AD350. Three of the coins, which were silver-plated, were declared treasure trove. We don't know very much about the Romans on Exmoor but it is quite likely that Iron-Age enclosures like Bat's Castle continued to be occupied into the Roman period and beyond.

No one has yet claimed Dunster as the site of Camelot but it does have its own King Arthur legend told in an early account of the life of St Carantoc, original patron of neighbouring Carhampton. The story goes that Carantoc, a Welsh monk, decided to choose an area for missionary work by throwing his portable altar stone into the Severn and following by boat to wherever it went ashore. Unfortunately he lost track of the stone and during his search of the West Somerset coast, came across Princes Cato and Arthur who were living at Dindrathrou (identified with Dunster). Nearby in the region of Carrum (Carhampton) a ferocious serpent was ravaging the land and was a threat to all. By this time Arthur had found the altar stone and thought it would make a good table but unfortunately anything placed on it was immediately thrown off. Carantoc enquired of the princes whether they had seen his altar stone and it was eventually restored to him once he had captured and tamed the serpent.

Whatever the tale's credibility, archaeological evidence indicates more and more that there was a settlement of some note in the Dunster area – perhaps to the east of Carhampton – during the period known as the Dark Ages.

The first Saxons invaded the area around AD700 and soon settled the present Dunster site. The first written reference came in the Domesday Book, which named the town Torre (tor) but it was probably called after a Saxon thane, Dunna, who founded the settlement around its central strategically placed hill. Tradition suggests that there was a Saxon fortress on the tor but there is no evidence of this. The last Saxon lord of Dunster was Aelfric who also held the neighbouring manor of Avill together with Bratton on the other side of Minehead. Alric held Broadwood while Algar held Alcombe and Minehead.

One of William of Normandy's chief supporters in his conquest of England was William de Mohun who came from St Lo, not far from Bayeux in Normandy. After the Battle of Hastings in 1066 William was granted 69 West-Country manors including Dunster where he decided to build his castle and which was to become the administrative centre of his estates.

Dunster was only a small manor. The Domesday survey of 1086 records only enough ploughland for one plough, five acres of meadow and 30 acres of pasture; 15 bordars (cottagers) with their families worked the strips of arable land in fields to the west of the town. However, two points indicate that the survey may not tell the whole story. The lord's tenants were expected to grind their corn at his mill. There are two mills mentioned in Dunster implying use by or for larger numbers than usual. Also, the value of the manor rose by 200 per cent, from 5s. in 1066 to 15s. in 1086, almost certainly because of the work and trade brought to Dunster by the building of the castle, details not asked for in the survey. The population of Dunster must have been much larger than the Domesday agricultural return implies.

William's choice of Dunster as the site for his castle was the making of the town. In 1197 it was described as a borough and by 1222 known to have a market. In 1253, Reginald de Mohun, the lord of the manor, granted the burgesses of Dunster the right to hold markets and fairs 'in North Street freely and quietly and fully' for ever. In return the burgesses gave him a tun (252 gallons) of wine worth 40s., perhaps pressed from grapes grown in the vineyards on the sunny south-facing slopes of Grabbist Hill.

The next year the burgesses were granted various privileges including some tax exemptions. Later charters granted the right to 'have furze, whorts, turfs, fern and heath sufficient for their fuel' on Croydon Hill, slime from the marsh (for improving their land) and common rights of pasture for their plough-cattle except on Estmersh. In addition, 40 acres were used as a rabbit warren and known as Coleborrowes. Coleborrowes replaced the old warren or 'coney-garth' on Conygar Hill from where the rabbits could all too easily reach and ravage the town's gardens. Rabbit was a welcome addition to the medieval diet but seems to have caused a problem at the time for burgesses were allowed to kill them freely so long as they took the skins to the castle.

Burgesses were those people who leased a burgage plot from the lord of the manor. These were long, narrow strips of land generally running at right angles to the street with enough ground for house, workshops and garden. The burgages in the High Street were separated on the east from the Hangar Park and on the west from Dunster Priory precinct, by a continuous wall or wooden paling. Many of the

Left: *Looking across the Deer Park to Grabbist Hill.*

Right: *Dunster from the air showing the burgage plots behind the houses on either side of the High Street.*

The stone wall on the right separates the burgage plots from the old Hangar Park, c.1865.

burgage plots can still be identified. Burgesses paid a rent to the lord of a shilling a year and a 'boroughright' or toll when a burgage plot was transferred. They were, in effect, free men, able to do what they liked with their burgage plots. They could bequeath them and prosperous tradesmen might acquire more than one in order to extend their businesses. The descriptive surnames of burgesses in 1266 show that by then the town was growing as a centre of craftsmanship and trade – Mazun, Smith, Carpenter, Poter, Baker, Webber, Fuller, Tanner, Corour (leather dresser), Glover, Chapman (pedlar), Millar, Gardiner, Fisher, Hunter, Dyer.

During this period sea-going ships harboured in the mouth of the River Avill – the area known as the Hawn or haven. They may even have navigated the tidal estuary of the Avill and tied up at the foot of the castle tor. The writer of *Gesta Stephani* in 1139 speaks of the impregnability of Dunster Castle, referring to it as 'inaccessible on the one side where it was washed by the tide and very strongly fortified on the other by towers and walls, by a rampart and outworks.'

Nearer the sea a creek known as the Northpulle (North Pill or river) ran through Foghelrismersh (Fowler's Marsh) and this may have been the site of the harbour. The people who lived in the cottages beside Marsh Lane and near the Hawn worked in maritime occupations such as boat building, sail-making and fishing and somewhere there must once have been a complex of wharves, storage cellars and workshops. In 1375, one of the 39 ships captured by the French in the Bay of Bourgneuf was the *St Marie Cog* of Dunster, said to have been built of oak from the castle park. These small ships carried cargoes of corn, wine, wool and leather. In 1418, the '*Leonard* of Dounsterre, barge of the noble lord the Lord Hugh Luttrell, Knight, Lord of Donnstre, whereof is master Philip Clapton' sailed to Bordeaux with a supply of live oxen to feed Hugh's men fighting in France. She returned with a cargo of French wine. In 1426 when the new gatehouse was built at the castle, 10,000 stone tiles were shipped in from Cornwall.

Fishing took place both on- and offshore. Foreshore fishing rights belonged to the lord of the manor and there were numerous fisheries, both weirs and pools, between Minehead and Blue Anchor. The weirs were usually well down the beach towards the low water tide mark and consisted of two lengths of low stone walling built in a V shape with each wall measuring some 100 to 200m in length and about 1.5m high. The apex pointed out to sea and at first wattles, and later baskets or nets, were placed across the neck. As the tide receded the water in the weirs ponded up and the fish were trapped. A similar method involved long rows of stakes with wattles or with nets stretched across. Both weirs and stakes demanded constant maintenance but the income from them was considerable and the right to hold one jealously guarded.

In the sixteenth century Dunster Haven (or

Hawn) was still a creek frequented by 'small botes' and in 1566 the *Mychael* 'of Donstarre', mastered by John Will, carried wool from Milford in Wales to Dunster. When Gerard of Trent visited Dunster in 1633 he noted the number of boats from Ireland visiting the 'pretty harbour'. Today no sign of the harbour itself remains for the whole river estuary has silted up.

Our newspapers these days are full of bad news and things that people have done wrong. Similarly many of the documents dating from the medieval period record the proceedings of the courts. The lord's steward always presided and a jury of 12 freemen attended the two principal courts held each year soon after Easter and Michaelmas. Borough officers were elected annually including two constables of the peace, two bread-weighers and two ale-tasters and later came keepers of the shambles and keepers of the streets. The constables reported all breaches of the peace, the bread-weighers presented bakers who sold bread of short weight and poor quality (perhaps adulterated with chalk) while the ale-tasters presented brewers whose beer was not up to scratch. Butchers and fishermen were expected to sell their goods in the local market and could be fined if they didn't. Among the responsibilities of the street-keepers was keeping them free of straying animals which, if impounded, could only be released on payment of a fee. Fines were imposed on those who broke the law.

The wide, open area in the centre of North Street (now High Street) was planned as a market square and by 1423 a range of open stalls had been built to augment the number of permanent shops and to provide for the ever-growing body of customers. Stallholders paid dues to the bailiffs while the keepers of the shambles, along with the other officers, helped regulate the business of the market. Offenders were tried at the pie-powder (dusty feet) court, which from 1426 was held in a wooden building that served as the Town Hall.

Some offences seem fairly petty but emerged from a real need to 'keep the peace' in an insular community. For example, in 1408 Ellen Watkyns was charged with being a common 'holcroppe' (petty pilferer) and a scold and disturber of the peace while in 1443 John Towker was presented as a 'common spy or listener at the windows of the neighbours and likewise a common nightwalker and eavesdropper.' In 1493 the wives of John Huyshe and Lenard Goldesmyth were named as quarrelsome and common gossips who were verging on scandal mongering. Their husbands were instructed to keep them in order!

Polluting the water supply, lighting bonfires near thatched houses, vandalism and gambling were all punishable offences and no one was exempt. We may well wonder what in 1410 caused Richard the chaplain of Lullokesburg (Luxborough) to 'draw the blood of Laurence Scolemayster with his fist'.

Dunster in c.1800 showing the wooden shambles and Town Hall in the centre of the street. The bell in the Yarn Market would be rung to announce that the market was open.

Chapter Two

WAR & PEACE

Dunster Castle from the Lawns, showing its fine strategic position. During the Civil War the Parliamentarians under Colonel Blake tried to capture the castle but were not successful.

Living beside a castle brought employment and prosperity. It also had its dangers. In 1138 Dunster Castle, held by William de Mohun for the Empress Matilda, was besieged and eventually reduced by Henry de Tracy on behalf of King Stephen. In 1265 during the barons' wars Sir William de Berkeley with a band of Welshmen landed at Minehead prepared to lay waste the region. Adam Gurdon, the warden of the castle and supporter of the baronial cause, led a rebel force and put the invaders to rout. After the defeat of the barons at the Battle of Evesham, Gurdon was himself ousted from the castle which at the time was held in wardship by Queen Eleanor.

During the Civil War between King and Parliament (1642–49) Dunster Castle was besieged over a period of months and the townspeople were inevitably caught up in the conflict. Dunster was a focal point of military activity in the West, with both Royalists and Roundheads keen to hold a fortress so well placed strategically. The castle was held initially by Thomas Luttrell for Parliament. He was not really a committed Parliamentarian himself but was married to a forceful wife, Jane, the daughter of Sir Francis Popham of Littlecote, a noted Parliamentarian. It was Jane who, in 1642, gave the order to open fire on a contingent of Cavaliers serving under Sir Ralph Hopton who were demanding the surrender of the castle, but Thomas himself ordered the removal of the rudders of ships in Minehead harbour to impede their getaway. However, after some skirmishes in the spring of 1643, Thomas was persuaded by Sir Francis Wyndham of Orchard Wyndham at Williton to join the Royalist cause and open the gates of the castle to the King's army. He paid over £1,000 to the cause, perhaps as a fine, perhaps as an earnest of his intentions but died early in the following year. His widow and son went to live at Marshwood in Carhampton.

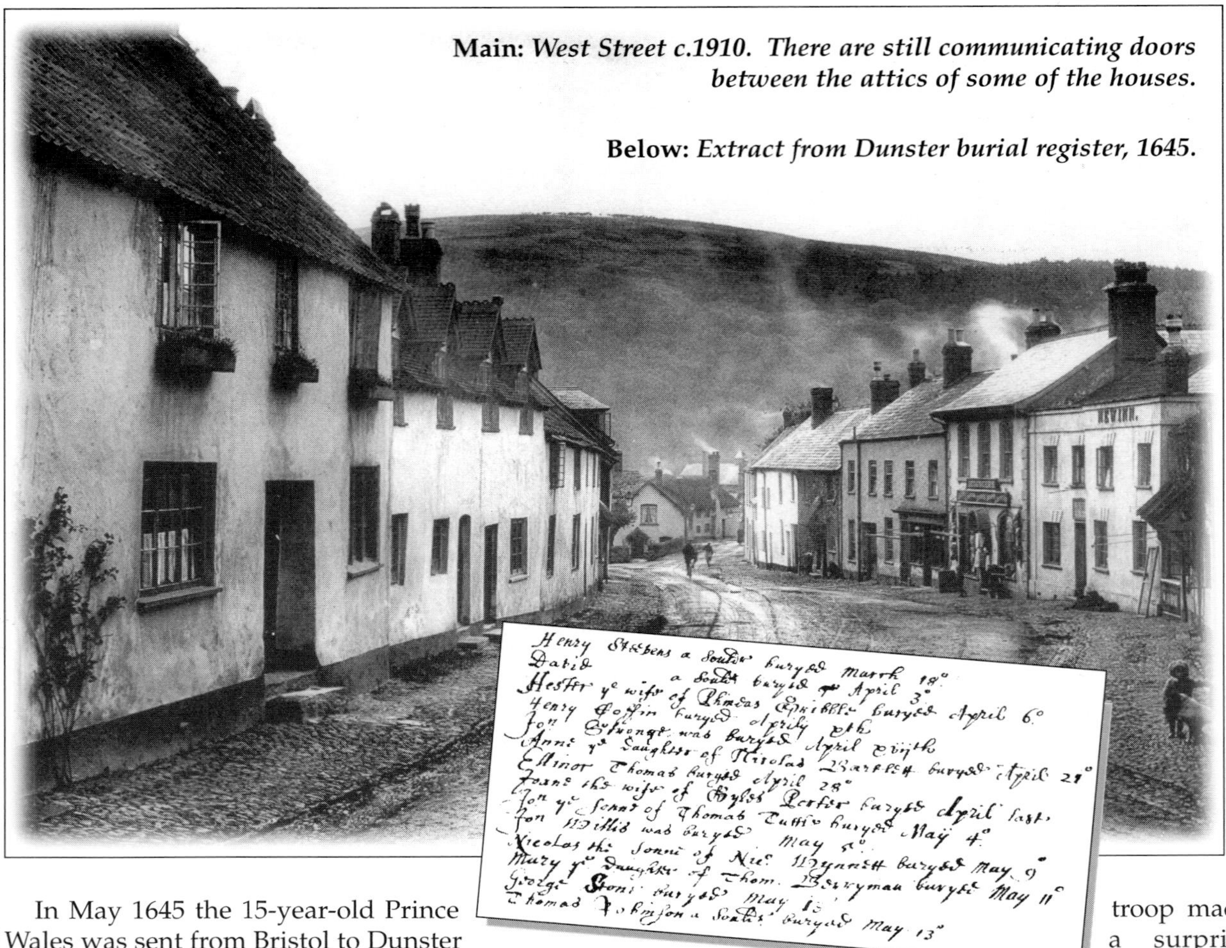

Main: *West Street c.1910. There are still communicating doors between the attics of some of the houses.*

Below: *Extract from Dunster burial register, 1645.*

Henry Steebens a Souldr buryed March 18°
David a Souldr buryed the April 3°
Hester ye wife of Thomas Gribble buryed April 6°
Henry Coffin buryed Aprill 7th
Jon Strange was buryed April eighth
Anne ye daughter of Nicolas Bartlett buryed April 21°
Ellinor Thomas buryed April 28°
Joane the wife of Gyles Porter buryed April last.
Jon ye sonne of Thomas Tutto buryed May 4°
Jon Willis was buryed May 5°
Nicolas the sonne of Nic° Wynnett buryed May 9°
Mary ye daughter of Thom. Berryman buryed May 11°
George Stone buryed May 13
Thomas Robinson a Souldr buryed May 13°

In May 1645 the 15-year-old Prince of Wales was sent from Bristol to Dunster to avoid the plague but his stay at the castle was brief since the disease was rife in Dunster itself, probably brought in by the army. During the same month, 23 burials are recorded. Many houses in West Street have communicating doors, which are said to date from this time when people avoided going into the street 'where they might contract the disease'.

In October 1645 Colonel Robert Blake, with 600 men, was ordered to Dunster to reduce the castle which was then being held for the King by its governor, Francis Wyndham. Blake made his headquarters in a 'strong house', the Ship Inn, now the Luttrell Arms Hotel. Although Wyndham was short of supplies and water he refused all Blake's demands for surrender and instead appealed to General Goring for reinforcements. Blake had no wish to storm the castle. He had drawn up his batteries behind the Ship Inn but even when he moved his trenches forward, his field guns were unable to make inroads in the massive medieval curtain walls and towers. Blake used miners from Mendip to undermine the walls in three places but still hesitated to fire. When ordered by Fairfax to do so, only one mine did any damage and that in such an inaccessible spot that Blake felt no compulsion to attack.

Meanwhile Francis Wyndham was hard pressed, not only for supplies but for ways of defending the weakened castle walls. Early in January a Royalist troop made a surprise attack on Blake in his 'strong house' and, outnumbering Blake's men, was able to destroy his 'trenches and batteries' and replenish Wyndham's supplies of powder and food. With their departure the siege continued.

The Royalists began to suffer defeat in the West Country and in mid-April, as rumours of Parliamentary successes began to reach the beleaguered men, it was decided by Blake and Fairfax that a final show of force might bring an end to the blockade. Blake and his men, with reinforcements totalling about 2,000, drew up in full battle array on May Hill facing the castle and summoned Wyndham to surrender. On 19 April Sir Francis accepted the generous terms offered. After a siege of more than five months, he and his men marched away from Dunster with drums beating, colours fluttering and musketeers at the ready, watched by soldiers from Cromwell's New Model Army and, surely with relief, by the townsfolk of Dunster.

The siege must have been a time of great anxiety for them with houses occupied, troops stationed on the hills close by and skirmishes in the town itself. It is said that 40 houses were burnt out during the siege and the Yarn Market was damaged. It was rebuilt in 1647. (It is claimed that a cannon ball hole can still be seen in one of the beams.) We know little of the opinions of the local

Hugh Luttrell's gatehouse was saved when the order to raze the castle to the ground was rescinded.

The Luttrell Arms Hotel. Traditionally the guest-house of the Abbot of Cleeve, the hotel was once three houses and was commandeered by Colonel Blake during the Civil War as his 'strong house'. By then it had become the Ship Inn and later in 1736 Richard Phelps, the Luttrells' 'artist in residence', painted a new sign which was resented by other landlords, led by Philip Harrison, and vandalised. By 1777 the inn was in ruins and was rebuilt as the Luttrell Arms Hotel. It became a coaching inn and meeting-place for village committees.

people but textile workers and seamen tended towards Puritanism and so often supported Parliament. The New Model Army was well disciplined and bought what provisions were needed. Some townsfolk may have done quite well by selling to the army and regretted the end of the siege but most, I expect, would have been glad to be free of the danger in their midst and the constant fear of what might happen next. At the end of the war Parliament ordered that the castle should be demolished and work began on razing the curtain wall but a last minute change of heart came just in time to save the dwelling house and Hugh Luttrell's gatehouse.

In 1685 the town was again involved in the thrill and horror of a national rebellion. In June that year the people's hero, the Protestant Duke of Monmouth, landed at Lyme Regis to challenge his Catholic uncle, James II, for the crown. As he marched north through Chard to Taunton where he was rapturously received, the Duke was joined by crowds of eager and naive working men whose enthusiasm was to be no substitute for arms and fighting skill when they met the King's army under Lord Feversham on the Somerset Levels. Twelve Dunster men, mainly substantial tradesmen, though their number included two doctors, joined Monmouth's march and were present at the disastrous defeat at Sedgemoor.

Of these men, Henry Luckwill, together with William Sully from Bridgwater, were hanged at Dunster. A third man, similarly sentenced, may have died of smallpox in prison. We can imagine the procession watched by silent and sympathetic townsfolk, as it made its way over the packhorse bridge to the gallows on Gallox Hill. Later the quartered bodies were 'disposed upon gates, bridges and crossways', a terrible reminder of the outcome of treachery.

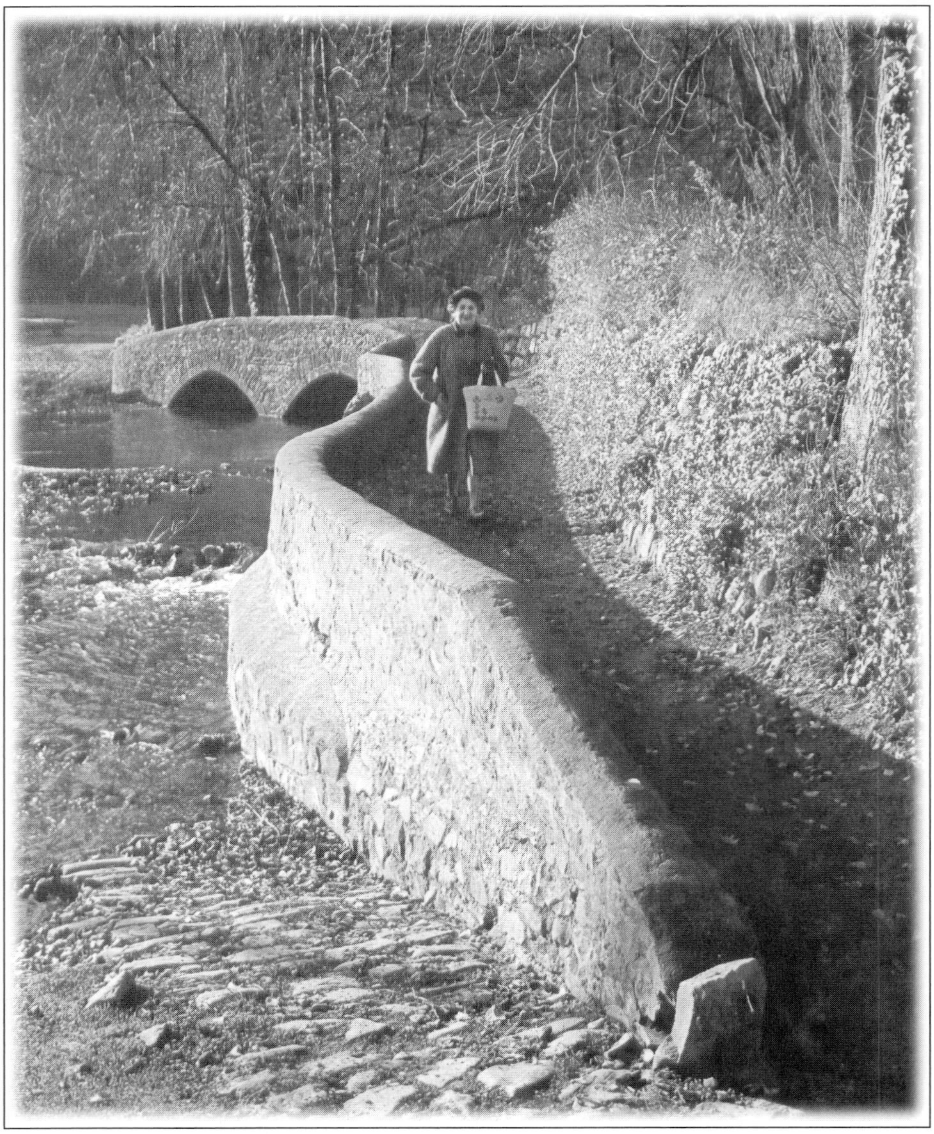

Mrs Chapman crosses the ancient packhorse bridge, known as Gallox Bridge.

Chapter Three

THE CLOTH TRADE

When John Leland visited Dunster on his travels around England in 1538, he noted that 'the toun of Dunestorre makith cloth'. In fact, more than 300 years earlier the woollen industry was well established in the town, as the occupations listed in an extent of 1266 show. For example, Adam the dyer, Walter the webber, William the fuller, Alice the webber and Christina the webber were all specialists in aspects of making cloth. This was an industry that involved a number of complex processes that in the medieval period were all 'hand crafts'.

First the wool was 'carded' or combed, before being spun on a distaff and spindle. The spinning-wheel came into use later. The yarn was then woven on a loom worked by hand and foot, and finally the resulting loose 'web' was fulled, again by hand or foot. Fulling involved beating the cloth in water, sometimes with the aid of fullers' earth, tallow or burned bracken that cleaned away the natural oils and shrank and felted the material. The cloth was then stretched out to dry in measured lengths held by tenterhooks on wooden racks or tenterbeds. Finally the cloth was finished; the nap was raised with teasles and sheared. Dyeing could be done at the yarn stage or after the cloth was woven; vegetable dyes were used including madder (red), sphagnum moss, weld (yellow) and woad (blue).

From the start families made cloth to clothe themselves but as specialisation developed so did the cloth industry. At first it was based in towns alongside other specialist crafts. Then, in the thirteenth century, the mechanisation of the fulling process, whereby the action of feet treading the cloth was replaced by a pair of pounding wooden hammers driven by a water-wheel, caused the industry to shift to rural areas where fast-running streams provided the water to power the wheels. It was probably for this reason that in the early 1200s the woollen industry expanded in Dunster; the first fulling mill is recorded in 1259.

By 1430 there were at least four fulling or tucking mills in Dunster, all of which were situated at the western end of the town where a leat already provided the water to drive the lord's corn mills. It appears that this leat was utilised by the new mills, for in 1376 William Taillour built a new fulling

Sheep provided the foundation for Dunster's medieval economy. This idyllic scene was photographed c.1910.

Pack-animals laden with bundles of cloth crossing Gallox Bridge.

mill over the lord's watercourse. Thomas Touker's mill was under Grabbist at Frackford and the Abbot of Cleeve had a mill in West Street, perhaps on the site where there was later a grist mill. Others were at unidentified sites – le Colverhay and Parlebienshey – but the name 'Toukerstrete' implies that they were all situated fairly closely together. A little later another mill was built on the river, east of the castle. Trade was good during the fifteenth century and in order to ensure the work got done fullers were ready to contravene the ordinance forbidding the mills to work on Sundays. During this period there were numerous 'tenting beds' or racks set out on the lower slopes of the castle tor and Grabbist Hill.

Little is known of the type of cloth that was produced in Dunster at this time. In 1431 Lady Margaret Luttrell bought 'fustyan' and 'tatterys' for a double gown for herself in 'the market place at

The Yarn Market, built by George Luttrell, c.1600.

Dunsterre'. She also bought linen cloth and russet cloth from William Stone who seems to have been a general merchant and may well have brought the cloth in from elsewhere. Accounts show that cloth was purchased from many different sources. There is also an order dated 1431 for a quantity of white cloth for 'the livery of my lady' which was evidently made locally since the weaving, fulling, dyeing and shearing are all itemised personally. John Dyer was also paid for dyeing a bed cover, hangings and cushions for 'my lady's hall and the chamber and the chapel at Karampton'.

Short cuts that lowered the quality of cloth produced in the town reflected on everyone's business and were punishable offences. William Morgan was charged with mixing 'flokkes' (flax) with the pure wool in his cloth while John Lenchelond used thistles instead of teasles to raise the nap. Dyeing was a messy and smelly business that needed a constant supply of clean water. With so many manufacturers using the same watercourse an order had to be made in 1492 forbidding the pollution of the lord's river with waste 'wodewater' before eight o'clock each evening. By dawn the dirty blue water would have flowed out to sea.

The organisation of the industry varied over the years but by the seventeenth century was centred around wealthy clothiers who had money to invest. There were independent spinners who bought their own wool and sold their own yarn direct to weavers at the Yarn Market built in Dunster round about 1600. Other spinners were employed by clothiers who bought and distributed the raw wool and collected the finished yarn. In the 1700s the yarn of spinners from Carhampton and Porlock was particularly prized. The yarn was woven by weavers who, in some places, banded together in guilds to enforce standards and for mutual protection. After the cloth had been fulled and dyed, clothiers would employ men to dress and finish the cloth. Sometimes the clothiers in Dunster leased fulling mills and racks and as such were responsible for nearly all the processes from raw wool to finished cloth. The will of the clothier Stephen Fox, who died in 1688, is one of several Dunster wills which mention racks, shears, pressing planks and other tools of the wool trade. These entrepreneurs went on to market the cloth and as a result their wills sometimes also mention shop counters, beam scales and weights and parchment skins for accounting.

Incidentally in Eamon Duffy's *The Voices of Morebath*, there is a tantalising reference to Sir Thomas Schorcum, a priest and maker of vestments, who lived in Dunster and who, in 1547, supplied a set of black vestments to Sir Christopher Trychay, parish priest of Morebath.

Various sorts of cloth were made in Dunster at different times but in 1607 an Act of Parliament laid down regulations which standardised the kersey-type cloth that took its name from the town. It stated that:

The Yarn Market in Dunster High Street, photographed by James Date, c.1880.

The Yarn Market in use by the WI during the Second World War.

> *... every broad cloth commonly called Tauntons, Bridgewaters and Dunsters made in the western part of Somersetshire, or elsewhere of like making, shall contain, being thoroughly wet, between 12 and 13 yards, and in breadth seven quarters of a yard at the least, and being well scoured, thicked, milled and fully dried, shall weigh 30 pounds the cloth at least.*

Broadcloth made on a broadloom needed two weavers to cope with the greater width.

Not long after George Luttrell built the Yarn Market, the woollen industry in Dunster seems to have suffered a setback and although there were periods of apparent recovery the overall trend for the future was downward. In 1621 a number of 'rackroomes' leased from George Luttrell were all said to be decayed yet in the middle of the century a piece of waste land was beaten out of rocks at the lower end of West Street below 'Rack Close' and used for more racks. The numbers of racks and value of their rents fluctuated but in spite of a few good years in the early 1700s the number gradually diminished. Racks were taken up and destroyed and well-established lessees such as John Perry and Nathaniel Ingram found themselves in arrears. They eventually gave their racks up. After 1764 racks no longer feature in the Luttrell rentals.

Nathaniel Ingram probably leased the grist mills in West Street that had been put up by Colle on the site of the Abbot of Cleeve's fulling mill and may have used them for fulling as well as grinding corn. When Henry Fownes Luttrell obtained the mill from Ingram in 1765 he converted it for fulling but by 1779 an initial annual return of £15 had fallen to £8.

Tracing the history of each fulling mill is complex and yields a far from complete picture. John Burnell leased the house and fulling mill at Frackford near the bridge in 1682 and William Leigh took over the same property in 1713. Both had the right to set up racks on Grabbist Hill. Members of the Hossom and the Coffyn families leased other fulling mills during this period.

The decline of the industry slowly but surely continued throughout the eighteenth century. Collinson, writing in 1791, spoke of 190 houses where there had once been 400 and of a near-defunct industry that had succumbed to competition from the North. As people moved away the mills and racks were given up. Sometimes the property and land was turned to other uses – in 1733 a mansion was built on the site of a fulling mill in West Street – but in some cases they were simply abandoned. Beside the road to Timberscombe not far beyond Frackford Bridge on the right-hand side is a copse in which can be seen all that remains of one of Dunster's fulling mills and of the leat bringing the water to power it.

Chapter Four

WORK & PLAY IN THE EIGHTEENTH CENTURY

Stray animals were penned in the pound and only released on payment of a fine.

During the sixteenth, seventeenth and early-eighteenth centuries when Dunster flourished as a market town and centre of the woollen industry there were other craftsmen with shops in the town besides clothiers, drapers and mercers. One of these was Edward Sweet, a silversmith, who, in the early 1700s occupied one of the old burgage holdings in the High Street that backed on to the Park or the Priory grounds. On 23 April 1719 Edward, along with other citizens 'having back doors out of each of our gardens belonging to the walls next and adjoining to the Parks and the Priory Ground', signed a deed agreeing to pay a shilling a year to the Luttrells as lords of the manor in respect of a right of way.

Sweet is mentioned in the records of the Dunster Borough Court Leet. At first he is referred to simply as a resident of the town but in the early 1720s he appears as a member of the jury. The Borough Leet was still responsible for overseeing the weekly market; ensuring that proper weights and measures were maintained and used; and investigating issues concerning cleanliness, health and even planning in the town.

During the time that Edward was serving on the twelve-man jury, the street-keepers presented James Wilkins junior and Philip Reed for 'laying of earth and dung in the street commonly called Middle Street to the annoyance of the inhabitants'; Hugh Matthews for 'building of a hog stye near his house in West Street' and William Phillips for 'washing of skins in the pott water'. Animals on the loose were a continuing problem and the pound was used to hold straying animals until claimed. No one, either rich or poor, could escape the rulings of the Borough Leet jury. On more than one occasion, the lord of the manor was presented for failing to maintain the pavement of Market (High) Street in proper condition and for not keeping in good repair the stocks, the pillory and the cucking-stool, 'instruments of justice'.

In 1710 Edward Sweet was assessed for land tax at 4s., the assessment being based on his stock in trade. While five other citizens were assessed at this rate, none was higher and it therefore seems that Edward was one of the wealthiest men in the town. In 1714 he took his turn as an overseer of the poor and during the same year was named as one of three churchwardens in Dunster. This is strange because it seems that he was a Dissenter, but 1714 was the year when a new silver paten was bought for Dunster Church, so perhaps Edward was 'co-opted' in order to assist in making this important purchase.

During the 1720s Sweet moved away from Dunster, maybe to Minehead where an Edward Sweet was buried in 1737. A Minehead will in that name was proved that year but it, like many other Somerset wills placed in the Exeter Record Office for safe keeping during the Second World War, was destroyed by enemy action.

Edward seems to have been a solid, educated and responsible citizen; a competent, provincial workman but with little flair. He was primarily a spoon maker, supplying the yeomen and entrepreneurs of West Somerset with the trefid spoons that were so popular at the time. Besides the spoons, the only other items known to bear Edward Sweet's mark are two candle-snuffer trays and a pair of snuffers. He was not called upon to make the new paten for the church when it was needed in 1714. Instead, the churchwardens bought one made by William Gamble of London.

The rich may have owned silver spoons but most ordinary people would have eaten their meals from earthenware plates. In the garden of the Luttrell Arms Hotel, situated beside the battery earthworks thrown up during the Civil War, is the shell of a recently restored pottery kiln. It is all that remains of a pottery run in conjunction with the Luttrell estate brickworks, which were established on the Warren around 1750. The pottery works were said to be 'in the old park' in 1759 and were doing good local business between 1758 and 1770.

In 1775 an advertisement for the pottery was placed in the Bristol newspapers.

> *A Pottery Work where is exceeding good clay and fuel plenty for making the coarse ware. Situated near several towns and above 20 miles distance from any other work of the kind, is to be lett. Or a good hand well-skilled in making and burning such goods and can be well recommended will meet with great encouragement to carry on this work by applying to George Gale at Dunster near Minehead in Somerset.*

The brick and pantyle yard was also advertised.

Although the pottery was offered on lease – an earlier advertisement specified seven or 14 years – it seems to have been worked by itinerant potters helped by local workmen. In 1758 Mr Symons, the potter, lodged in Dunster for just over three weeks and in 1761 the expenses were paid of James Norris, 'a potter coming from Crock Street to take the work'. The potters were paid for the work they did; lodgings were provided when necessary and there was a generous liquor supplement for everyone, which was augmented during the very thirsty work of firing the kiln or 'burning'.

The potter was a highly skilled person, responsible for all aspects of the work: digging the clay, making the goods, supervising the building, packing and firing kilns, delivering goods to individuals and local retailers and packing goods ready for shipping to wholesalers.

John and Ruth Mogg of Bristol prepared and fired seven kilns between 1759 and 1760 and Ruth managed a shop where the finished goods were sold. They produced a wide range of domestic

Dunster pottery kiln, following recent renovations. The kiln is shown in a landscape painting at the castle dated 1765. It is thought to be the oldest extant kiln in the country.
(Photograph courtesy of Exmoor National Park Authority.)

earthenware including platters, pots and porringers, pitchers and pitkins, not to mention bowls for washing and pans for commodes. There were special pots for preserving laver, that seaweed delicacy once so popular on the Bristol Channel coast, for pickling vegetables and other pots to be used in the making of butter and cream.

Following John's death – he was buried in Dunster on 21 November 1760 – his wife was left to settle up the business and accounts with Henry Fownes Luttrell. Mogg may have been responsible for the brickyard as well as the pottery, for both were advertised to let in 1760.

The pottery may have been given up quite quickly but the brickyard at the Warren continued to be run as a profitable venture until about 1919, making bricks, tiles and pipes at competitive prices, for use in many local building enterprises.

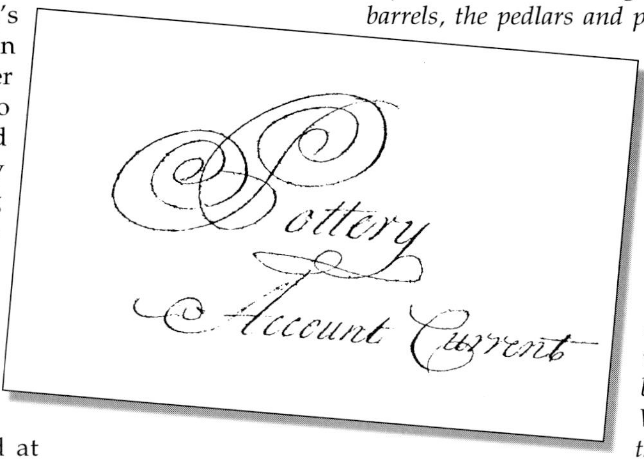

Cover of the pottery account book, 1759–60.

For several centuries the high spot of the year for many of Dunster's inhabitants would have been the annual fair. In her unpublished article, 'A Backward Look at the Market and Midsummer Fair in Dunster', Eleanor Crane wrote:

The eager visitor to the Fair could buy bread and cakes, breeches and bonnets, earthenware and silver, cutlery and hardware. She or he could replenish her store of rope, thongs and laces, saddlery and pewter; she could have pots and pans repaired by the brazier and the pewterer, buy shoes or boots, gloves and hats. The cooper was there selling fine buttertubs and water barrels, the pedlars and piddlers with their baskets of ribbons, lace, stockings and buttons. Toys for the children, confectionery and gingerbread stalls were there in plenty, as were sellers of books and tobacco, fresh fruit and fish. Occasionally, there was a visit by a travelling quack doctor, and when the season was good, women with baskets full of nuts for sale. When the marketing was done there was the fun of the fair to be enjoyed and marvelled at. Puppet and other shows amused the children, who readily gave their small money to dip into the Lucky Bag or spin round on the Whirligig. A man with a wild beast or a bear was sure to appear, and the lotteries and the Will of the West show amused child and adult alike. Bullocks and sheep, penned at the end of the Market Street, added their own sight, sound and smell to the cheerful mêlée of the Midsummer Fair.

The old Town Hall and shambles, c.1800.

Butter Cross

The ancient Butter Cross stood originally at the crossroads between Church Street and High Street. It was moved in the 1800s to make way for increasing traffic. The date and initials, WC 1871 WS, probably refer to its renovation. Climbing the hill behind is Conduit Lane leading to the medieval holy well of St Leonard, which may have provided the water supply for the priory and for the arched water-trough which once stood in the south wall of the churchyard.

With the decline in the woollen industry, fewer people visited Dunster market and by 1800 the fair sold little in the way of essentials and had become simply a fun fair. In 1765 Minehead Turnpike Trust had been set up by some of the local gentry, including Henry Fownes Luttrell, partly in the hope that new and improved roads would counteract the decline in industry and trade, prevalent in the whole area. A new turnpike road was built from Minehead through Alcombe to Dunster, and then on via Timberscombe, Beazley and Lype to Bampton. Other links were made with the Bridgwater and Taunton turnpikes but it was too late.

Streets and bridges fell into disrepair and the shambles in the centre of the High Street became so dilapidated that in 1825 it was pulled down. The old Town Hall, Tub House, Corn Cross and stocks all disappeared although the Butter Cross was re-erected later beside the Alcombe road where medieval Dean Lane meets Back Lane. The Yarn Market remained; a picturesque symbol of the past, its preservation hinting at Dunster's future.

Right: *Newmylle and Nethermylle were united under one roof by 1620.*

Dunster Mill

Corn mills at Dunster are first mentioned in Domesday Book when two mills worth 10s. to the lord of the manor, William de Mohun, were recorded. The mill played an important part in the economy of the medieval manor, all tenants having to take their corn to the lord's mill to be ground while the mill would be leased to a miller who would take a percentage of the corn ground for himself.

In 1329 the two mills were known as Overmylle and Nethermylle and were leased to a burgess, Walter Rughe, for an annual rent of £16. In 1405 the rent was set at £10 on the condition that the lessee

Dunster Mill at the turn of the twentieth century.

A drawing on the cover of George Gale's account book 1778–79 which gives details of repairs to Dunster Mill.

was responsible for all repairs. Then in 1427 William Person who already leased the older mills built Newmylle. By 1620 Newmylle and Nethermylle were united under one roof on the present mill site and known as Lower Mill. Overmylle or Higher Mill was presumably further upstream but had disappeared by 1779.

In March of that year the mill lease was advertised and included:

All those complete set of Grist Mills known by the name of Dunster Mills with a very good newly erected dwelling house thereto adjoining and also proper stabling, Hogsty and other useful conveniences.

A most condescending application was made by Daniel Heald of Spittlegate who referred to Dunster as 'a little country place with nothing of a flour mill'. His offer of £5 a year annual rent was given short shrift by George Gale, the Luttrell agent, who soon negotiated a lease with a Mr Mills of Bristol who was to be allowed to make the improvements and alterations he wished as long as he always remembered that Dunster Mill was in full view of the park and that Mr Luttrell expected alterations to be done 'uniform' and 'agreeable to his good liking'. The mill, together with the nearby bridge and adjoining arch, formed a picturesque feature in Henry Fownes Luttrell's landscaping of the castle grounds.

Comprehensive repairs to the mill began in 1779 and were completed three years later but Mr Mills did not stay to reap the benefits. The lease passed to John Bryant in 1782 and in 1801 to John Harvey who in 1802 insured the mills for £2,500. A valuation made in 1838 reflected a slump in trade:

It is clear that trade has suffered because of the erection of new flour mills in the neighbourhood which have deprived Mr Harvey of many of his best corn dealers, causing reduction in trade.

The mill remained in the Harvey family until 1875 when the business was taken over by Thomas Evered.

The profitable running of a water-mill depends on a regular supply of water and this had always been a matter for dispute in Dunster. There are several ordinances dating to the second half of the fifteenth century forbidding people to throw anything into the stream that might block the flow during the working week. The pressure of demand on water by the numerous fulling mills and dyehouses limited the flow to the corn mills, positioned almost last on the leat, and rights to water were sometimes questioned. In 1721 there was a long drawn out dispute over the supply to Madam Luttrell's Mault Mill and Tyrrol's Tucking Mill. Evidently the tucking mill would not work when the malt mill-wheel was running.

In 1883 a long-standing wrangle between the Dunster miller and the Wynch family at Knowle House who, in summer, diverted water for irrigation, came to a head. The final straw came one day when yet again there was no water and the stones at the mill ground to a halt. William Evered, who managed Dunster Mills for his father, strode up to Knowle House in a fury, in order to open the sluices. His greatest crime, as set out in a letter from Colonel Wynch to Mr Luttrell, was not that he interfered with the irrigation at Knowle House, but that he walked in front of the drawing-room windows in full view of the Colonel's guests.

The lord's leat carried water to drive the town's mills.

Gradually the mill was worked less and less. In 1909 H.C. Maxwell-Lyte, Dunster's erudite historian, remarked: 'The wheels often stand idle nowadays, the lessee James Phillips having a more important mill at Minehead.' Long before this the mill in its picturesque setting had become the haunt of artists and photographers. Even the austere Henry Maxwell-Lyte waxed near lyrical in his description of the mill: 'Nestling amid lofty trees immediately under the precipitous slope of the Tor, and close to a clear

Dunster Mill, c.1900.

stream fringed with dock leaves and meadowsweet'. In the late 1930s visitors paid half-a-crown for 'permission to sketch in Mill Walk'.

The necessity for national self-sufficiency during the Second World War led to the repair and reopening of the mill. A bakery on the premises, which in the 1930s had been run by the Cockrem brothers who delivered hot rolls in the town in the early morning, supplied bread baked with local flour to both castle and town. When peace came, the mill was confined to grinding for animal feed. It closed in 1962 and in 1975 was given to the National Trust by Colonel Walter Luttrell.

The mill stood, silent and neglected, until it was leased in 1979 to Laura and Arthur Capps who, aided by grants from the Manpower Services Commission, the Historic Buildings Council for England and the National Trust, supervised a restoration to working order. The mill was opened to the public in February 1980.

Chapter Five

The Nineteenth Century

Dunster High Street, c.1865, before the restoration of the castle. To the left is the Luttrell Arms Hotel. Part way down the street, putts stand outside the butchers' shambles built in 1825. A little further on is the house used as a school, once Lock's Café and later the Bantam Shop.

By clearing away the remnants of Dunster's earlier greatness, the town was in a position to develop in new directions. In 1840 the *Somerset Gazette Directory* noted that as the former wool trade was wholly lost the population was 'dependent upon the retail business of the neighbourhood'. According to Greenwood, writing in 1822, of the 183 families in the town, 84 were involved in agriculture, 78 in trade, manufacture and handicraft and 21 in other occupations. *Pigot's Directory* of 1830 lists bakers, blacksmiths, butchers, carpenters, coopers, maltsters, millers, saddlers, tailors, tallow-chandlers, watchmakers and wheelwrights to whom can be added from *Bragg's Directory* (1840) dressmakers, a straw-bonnet maker, tea dealer, nursery and seedsman and a chinaman. Versatility was the order of the day. William Vicary, postmaster, was also Parish Clerk and hairdresser; William Letty, auctioneer and clock-maker, was agent for Atlas Fire Insurance and for the *Somerset County Gazette*, while Worthington Vesey Prideaux, who began life as a plumber, later took over the Post Office.

By 1840 Dunster had clearly turned her back on the old days of the cloth industry and weekly market and was developing as a town of small businesses ready to serve the local neighbourhood.

A few families saw little prospect of success and left Dunster to seek their fortunes in Australia. Following the death of Thomas Markham, tailor and innkeeper, his widow Mary decided, at the age of 60, to emigrate with her children: John, a saddler, whose wife Georgiana came from Porlock; Henry, an agricultural labourer, and Margaret, a general servant. They were all able to read and write and we know that John and his wife were Wesleyan Methodists. They sailed on 14 September 1851 on board the *Statesman*, bound for Geelong in Victoria. Two years later another son, Thomas, a carpenter, with his wife,

Dunster Schools

Right: *Dunster School soon after opening in 1872.*

Left: *The front of the Wesleyan School premises in Mill Lane, now a private house.*

Right: *Dunster School, 1911. Pupils include Jack Parham* (second row, fifth from left) *and Reg Vaulter* (front row, fourth from left).

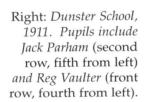

Left: *The Chapel School, Mill Lane, c.1900. Arthur Dyer* (fair boy standing middle front); *Daisy Court* (third from right back school row).

Elizabeth, and three children sailed on the *Stebonheath* to Newtown. In January of the same year, James Tudball, another Wesleyan from Dunster, travelled with his wife, Hannah, through appalling flooding on the Somerset Levels to Deptford, where they embarked on the *Monteagle*, bound for Melbourne, to work for Captain Buckley of Flemington. Their son, William Henry, was born in Cotham in 1855.

It is highly likely that these literate Wesleyan adventurers were among the first working people of Dunster to receive a regular education. In 1818 the vicar of Dunster, the Revd G.H. Leigh, stated in the parochial return: 'no school in this parish, poorer classes would be grateful for education'. Six years later, William Moore, a respected Methodist preacher, left £800 to found a day school in Dunster. It was opened in premises in Mill Lane, close to the chapel, built in 1811, and manse, and when a new chapel was built in West Street in 1839, the school expanded into the old chapel buildings. It was the first Wesleyan day school in West Somerset and one of the first to receive a government grant and regular inspection. The school thrived and in 1853 it was enlarged to accommodate 60 pupils.

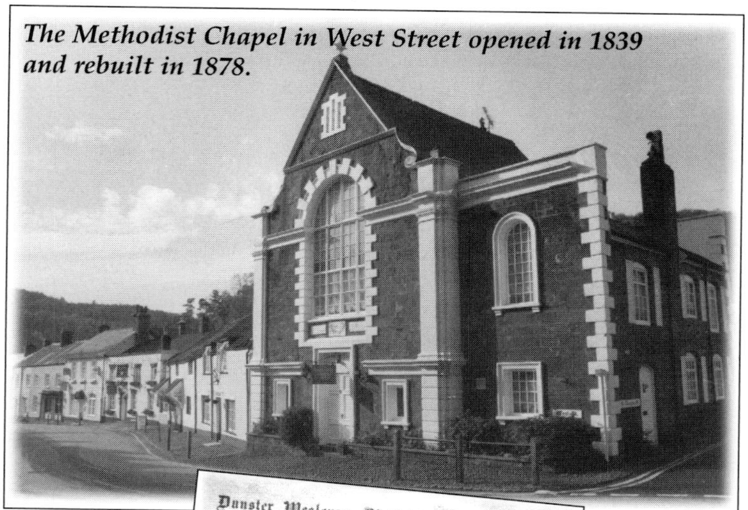

The Methodist Chapel in West Street opened in 1839 and rebuilt in 1878.

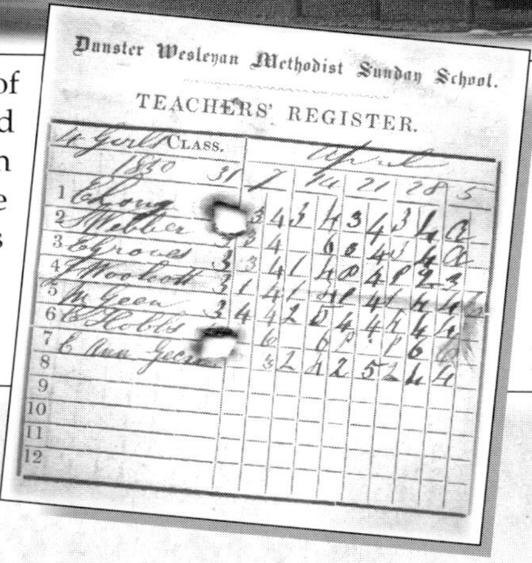

One or two small private, or 'dame', schools educated a handful of children in the town. In addition, there were a number of small private boarding schools, and Miss Elizabeth Harvey's Academy for Young Ladies was open for more than 20 years, teaching boarding pupils from some distance. However, it was the opening of the Wesleyan School that seems to have galvanised the Establishment into action.

Priory Farm, looking from the site of the old vicarage towards the castle before it was restored, c.1865. Note the straw rick raised on staddle stones.

By 1830 a Charity School had been set up in Dunster, supported by the Luttrell family and with Mary Strong as schoolmistress. In 1851 John Jones and his wife, Ann, were master and mistress, and the school was probably occupying premises on the eastern side of the High Street. The school became known as Dunster Church of England National School and in April 1863, Thomas Moore, a certificated teacher and principal of the school, started to keep a daily record of its progress. This log reflects his struggle to teach basic reading, writing, ciphering and religious instruction against the odds of consistent absences for potato-planting and picking, stone-clearing and bird-scaring, as well as haymaking, harvesting, mushrooming, gleaning and picking worts – a reminder that half of Dunster's families were still employed in agriculture and needed to supplement meagre incomes in every way possible.

Special occasions involved the master, too, and at a time when education was not compulsory, the school might be closed for ploughing matches, Minehead Hurdle Races, cricket week on the Lawns, Club Walks and Dunster Great Market. A visit by Womwell's Menagerie in July 1869 caused a sensation, not least because the management refused to pay the turnpike toll and the elephant lifted the gate off its hinges to let them all through. Parish feasts to celebrate national events were held as early as 1856 when one was provided for the people of Dunster to mark the end of the Crimean War.

Education was an issue close to the heart of the vicar, the Revd T.F. Luttrell. He supported and taught in the school and ran a night school for boys and young men where they could learn to read. 'In the evening of his life', he 'signified his determination to build schools and a teacher's residence for the educational requirements of the Parish.' He was encouraged by Mr George Luttrell who gave the site and contributed to the costs. In 1872 the school was able to move from the High Street to its spacious new premises near the church. Unfortunately the vicar did not live to see the opening of the new site. In honour of the occasion, 130 children, preceded by a banner that was inscribed 'Dunster Church Schools', marched from their old school through the churchyard to the new schoolroom.

The school prospered, with pupils walking in from Carhampton and Withycombe to take advantage of its high standards. Gradually numbers at the Wesleyan School dwindled and in 1903 it was closed. The 20 remaining pupils were transferred to the National School.

The new school was only one of a number of building projects begun at this time. The castle was re-modelled, the Parish Church thoroughly restored and the Wesleyan Chapel rebuilt. The police station and magistrates' court at the foot of Dunster Steep was built in 1858 and the village hospital opened in 1867. The West Somerset Railway was extended to Minehead in 1874 and a station built at Dunster Marsh. Several of the larger houses were reconstructed with new frontages and a few new houses were built. These schemes brought an influx of workmen and new opportunities for employment. Dunster's population rose from 983 in 1831 to 1,156 in 1871 and directories record increased numbers in building and related trades.

Dunster was a popular venue for artists from the late 1700s onwards.

Most of the property in Dunster belonged to the Luttrells and although there were some excellent houses, others suffered from age and needed money spending on them, as Mr G.F. Luttrell found when he inherited the estate in 1867. Mr Ponsford, his agent, reporting to a government commission investigating the working conditions of women and children in agriculture in 1867, made it clear that landowners who felt a responsibility to provide decent accommodation for their low-paid tenants could not expect to make a profit from their property. One house in neighbouring Minehead recently bought by Mr Luttrell for £80 had an annual rent of £5. After repairing it, he still felt that he should reduce the rent

Rose Cottage, Dunster. It is hard to imagine these picturesque cottages as anything but good!

The New Vicarage

The new vicarage – known as the Priory – and the men who built it, 1875.

to £3. New cottages with three bedrooms were being built in Minehead using good local stone and slate from the quarry at Treborough but there were few such new cottages in Dunster where property at the time tended to be old and varied in quality. George Long, a labourer, and his wife had one room downstairs, a small back house and two rooms upstairs for themselves and their four children. James Long, pig killer, lived in two good rooms down and two up in part of the old workhouse which had been turned into cottages. William Long, mason and Parish Clerk, had two good downstairs rooms and three up and was even able to take a lodger. William Davey, carter, had a large, roomy thatched cottage with an excellent garden running down to the river, though on occasion it flooded right up to the door.

In contrast was the cottage, one up, one down, for which the Gill family paid an annual rent of £3. When the commissioner called, the mother was out in the fields and an untidy daughter was looking after her blind grandmother. The front door and staircase were shared with the next-door house where a child lay ill with measles. It was a 'very bad cottage'. Further on, Court, a machine wright, lived in 'a wretched looking house', nearly bare of furniture, just one room up and one down for the husband who drank, his wife in rags and five or six children.

The last 30 years of the century were a time of some prosperity for the town with retailers, wholesalers and craftsmen taking full advantage of the economic boom initiated largely by Mr Luttrell's investment in building projects – school, church, new vicarage as well as some houses.

With their rising standard of living many looked to improve the amenities of the town and in this they received every encouragement, financial and otherwise, from Mr Luttrell. Streets were surfaced, water was piped to the town from Broadwood, and gas and electricity were laid on. By the end of the century the streets were lit in winter by 30 oil lamps. In 1825 a new butchers' shambles had been built in the High Street near the Luttrell Arms Hotel and in 1874 a Reading Room was opened above it – newspapers were provided and a library of some 200 volumes made

The High Street

Above: *Dunster High Street, c.1875.*

Below: *The Annual Feast of the Ancient Order of Foresters.*

available to the parish. The opening of the railway provided new links with Minehead, Taunton and beyond while the daily coach between Minehead and Williton continued to call at the Luttrell Arms. The carrier called each weekday, adapting to the new form of transport by connecting with the statutory 'Parliamentary' train at Williton. The weekly journey to Exeter involved an overnight stop.

Not everybody was prosperous. From 1834 Dunster was part of the Williton Union and paupers were sent to the grim workhouse there. A number of Friendly Societies provided mutual support and a form of insurance against illness or injury, with members paying a small weekly subscription and receiving benefit when unable to work. Dunster Tradesmen's Club owned a field between Frackford and Gallox Bridge that was leased to augment their income. A young men's Friendly Society was set up in 1871 and the Ancient Order of Foresters was well established by the 1870s when they held their annual walk and feast in the High Street.

The Dunster and Minehead Village Hospital, West Street, c.1870. Formerly a private residence owned by the Luttrells, the hospital reverted to that status in 1920 and is now known as Grabbist House.

In 1858 a new police station and magistrates' court was built at the bottom of Dunster Steep with living accommodation for a superintendent and sergeant.

In the early 1860s a number of people including the vicar of Dunster, the Revd T.F. Luttrell, and the rector of Wootton Courtenay, Bishop Chapman, met at Dunster and decided to form a small hospital and dispensary there 'for the relief of the poor of the neighbourhood in cases of accident and sickness.'

Following this meeting in 1867 the Dunster and Minehead Village Hospital was opened with five beds in a property leased from Mr Luttrell on the sloping ground to the west of West Street, formerly known as Happy Valley. The first matron was Mrs Govier who was paid a salary of £20 a year and was the only trained nurse. She must have had servants to help her. The honorary secretary at the time was the vicar of Carhampton, the Revd W.P. Michell who worked untiringly to make the little hospital a success. The honorary medical staff included at first Dr Charles Roberts who was

The police station and magistrates' court built in 1858 with living accommodation for a superintendent and sergeant.

Samuel Ell

Samuel Ell was a man of many parts. Besides being the dispenser for the hospital he ran an Aladdin's Cave of a shop where all sorts of medicaments for both humans and animals were sold as well as home-made marmalade (served in the House of Lords) and a 'celebrated algae sauce prepared from Betty Webber's laver [which] combined with several other wholesome stomachics render it a most delicious and agreeable relish, far superior to most other sauces.'

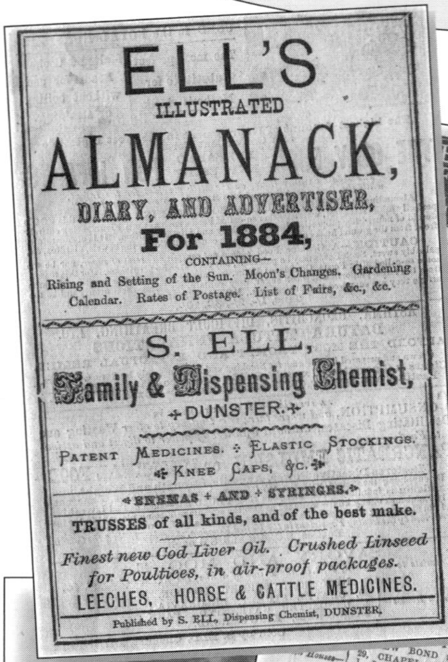
ELL'S
ILLUSTRATED
ALMANACK,
DIARY, AND ADVERTISER,
For 1884,
CONTAINING—
Rising and Setting of the Sun. Moon's Changes. Gardening Calendar. Rates of Postage. List of Fairs, &c., &c.
S. ELL,
Family & Dispensing Chemist,
DUNSTER.
PATENT MEDICINES. ELASTIC STOCKINGS. KNEE CAPS, &C.
ENEMAS AND SYRINGES.
TRUSSES of all kinds, and of the best make.
Finest new Cod Liver Oil. Crushed Linseed for Poultices, in air-proof packages.
LEECHES, HORSE & CATTLE MEDICINES.
Published by S. ELL, Dispensing Chemist, DUNSTER.

BEST FOOD FOR INFANTS
USED in the ROYAL NURSERIES
The most perfect Substitute for Mother's Milk.
Malted & Cooked Ready for use without boiling or straining.
FOOD PREPARED EXPRESSLY FOR INFANTS.
TIS, DIFFICULT BREATHING, ETC.
ATULA INHALATIONS
ROMPT AND EFFECTUAL RELIEF.
ION, or MEDICINAL FOOD,
Appetite, Strength and Weight.
D MOORE,
BOND STREET, LONDON, W.
Sold by S. ELL, Chemist, DUNSTER.

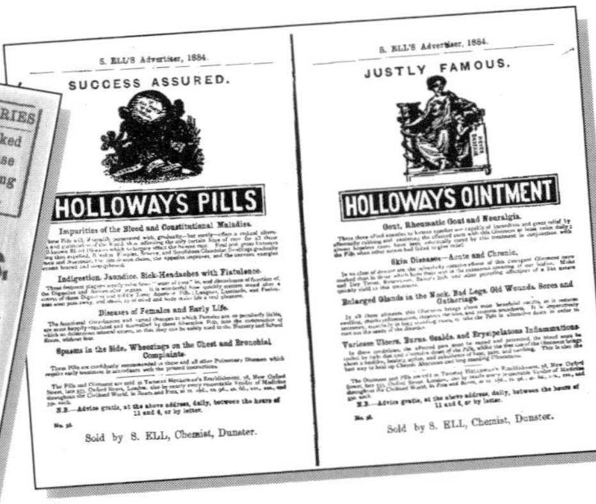
S. ELL'S Advertiser, 1884.
SUCCESS ASSURED.
HOLLOWAY'S PILLS
Impurities of the Blood and Constitutional Maladies.
Indigestion. Jaundice. Sick-Headaches with Flatulence.
Diseases of Females and Early Life.
Spasms in the Side, Wheezings on the Chest and Bronchial Complaints.
N.B.—Advice gratis, at the above address, daily, between the hours of 11 and 4, or by letter.
Sold by S. ELL, Chemist, Dunster.
S. ELL'S Advertiser, 1884.
JUSTLY FAMOUS.
HOLLOWAY'S OINTMENT
Gout, Rheumatic Gout and Neuralgia.
Skin Diseases—Acute and Chronic.
Enlarged Glands in the Neck, Bad Legs, Old Wounds, Sores and Gatherings.
Varicose Ulcers, Burns, Scalds, and Erysipelatous Inflammations.
N.B.—Advice gratis, at the above address, daily, between the hours of 11 and 4, or by letter.
Sold by S. ELL, Chemist, Dunster.

Edgar Dyer used to tell of an incident concerning Samuel Ell. A man from outside the village paid a visit to the village doctor. After examining him the doctor wrote out a prescription and said, 'Go to Ell', but the poor man, not knowing the local chemist, thought he said, 'Go to Hell' – hardly an encouragement for a sick person!

CHEMICAL FOOD,
Or Syrup of the Phosphates of Iron, Lime, Potash and Soda.
Prepared from the formula of Mr. Edward Parrish, of Philadelphia.
TRY ELL'S
CHILBLAIN LINIMENT,
FOR UNBROKEN CHILBLAINS.
It will give relief in Five Minutes.
Prepared and sold by
S. ELL, Dispensing Chemist, DUNSTER.

Above: *Samuel Ell outside his shop in Church Street, c.1885.*

succeeded, when he moved away, by Dr Thomas Clark, joined in 1882 by Dr Francis Hayes. In 1879, 600 subscribers presented Dr Clark with £150 as 'a slight recognition of the long and valuable services gratuitously rendered by him' to the hospital.

A dispenser was appointed annually and, following Mr Attwater and Mr Penrose in 1873, Samuel Ell held this position until his death in 1910. He was frequently praised for his services though his honorarium never seems to have exceeded £12 a year. After his death Mrs Ell became the dispenser.

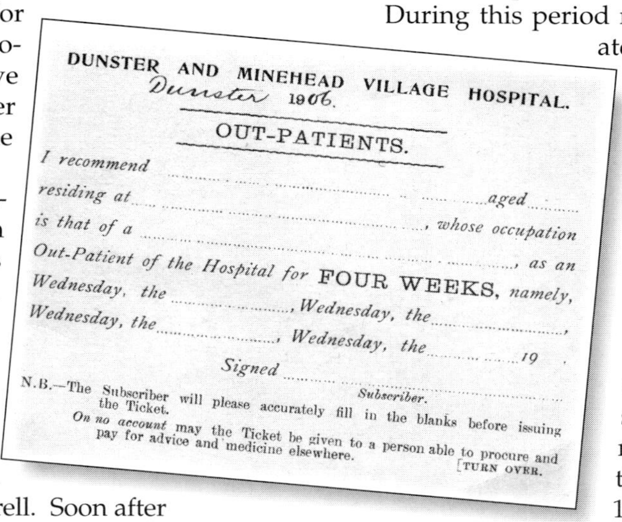
DUNSTER AND MINEHEAD VILLAGE HOSPITAL.

Dunster 1906.

OUT-PATIENTS.

I recommend ....

residing at .... *aged* ....

is that of a ...., *whose occupation*

.................., *as an*

Out-Patient of the Hospital for FOUR WEEKS, *namely,*

Wednesday, the ...., *Wednesday, the* ....,

Wednesday, the ...., *Wednesday, the* .... *19* .

Signed .... *Subscriber.*

N.B.—The Subscriber will please accurately fill in the blanks before issuing the Ticket.

On no account may the Ticket be given to a person able to procure and pay for advice and medicine elsewhere.

[TURN OVER.

Subscriptions, donations, collections from churches and other bodies and special events financed the hospital including, for many years, the proceeds from the opening of Dunster Castle Gardens. Subscriptions in 1868 amounted to £111.6s.8d. headed by £15 from Mr Luttrell. Soon after this he decided to give the premises rent-free in lieu of a subscription. The usefulness of the hospital was soon appreciated. In 1868 the annual report stated that, 'If any doubt of the necessity for an institution of this kind existed the experience of the past year may set it to rest, never has the hospital been so completely full.'

Both inpatients and outpatients were accepted, outpatients being able to attend the free dispensary for treatment. Inpatients at first seem to have been people with long-term complaints. Labourers, farm servants and the really needy could be recommended for treatment by subscribers who, for an annual donation of 10s., might recommend one outpatient a year and, for £1, two outpatients and one inpatient. The hospital catered for surrounding parishes as far apart as Porlock and Luxborough, and the clergy there were able to recommend patients. During the first year 105 patients were treated, 18 being inpatients; by 1901 there were 35 inpatients and 183 outpatients.

During this period numbers of patients fluctuated and the number of beds in the hospital increased. One thing was certain – the hospital was much appreciated. In 1893 a mortuary was built on the site of the old coal house and a probationer nurse was appointed for the first time to assist the matron. In 1900 a new ward was made for male patients and surgical operations grew in number as medical expertise developed. In the early 1900s there were 11 cases in which adenoids were removed, and appendicitis was mentioned for the first time. By this time the matron's salary had risen to £40. However, financial problems, the growing inadequacy of the building and the removal of the outpatients from the system following the introduction of the 1913 National Insurance Act led to the decision that the hospital should be moved to Minehead. In 1920 the cottage hospital at Dunster closed, handing over to the new Luttrell Memorial Hospital at Minehead.

Left: *Looking across to the new vicarage c.1870 from the castle. In the foreground are the castle stables and the Home Farm barns. In the centre are walled gardens with fruit trees, some trained against the walls, with the Priory Farm cattlesheds to the left of the dovecot and tithe barn behind. Note the Perpendicular east window in the church – it was taken out during the restoration.*

Right: *Haybarn at Home Farm.*

Right: *Dunster haymakers, c.1930.*

Above: *Building a rick in the field behind Sea Lane Bungalow. Ted Early and his son Ron, c.1950.*

In 1896 the decision was taken to form a fire brigade at the castle and donations were solicited from insurance companies for the purchase of uniforms. The Imperial contributed £10 and the Norwich Union, three guineas. After receiving advice from the London Fire Brigade, uniforms were bought at two guineas a head including belt and axe. Only the officers seem to have had helmets together with silver buttons and red cuffs. Mr Davis, the Captain, had red facings to his tunic. The appliance with all the necessary hoses and standpipes was kept in the coach-house in the castle grounds. A board that once hung in the Tithe Barn listed the members of the brigade at the end of the century.

During the nineteenth century nearly half the population of Dunster was still employed in agriculture. People worked both on the outlying farms such as Broadwood and Higher Marsh and on the farms still in the heart of the village – Priory Farm right beside the church and Home Farm, the farm at the castle. It was, in spite of setbacks, still the prime economic activity in the area.

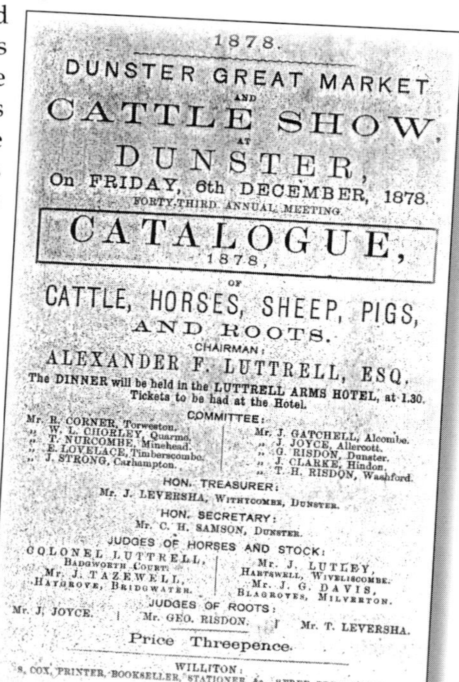

1878.

DUNSTER GREAT MARKET
AND
CATTLE SHOW,
AT
DUNSTER,
On FRIDAY, 6th DECEMBER, 1878.
FORTY-THIRD ANNUAL MEETING.

CATALOGUE,
1878,
OF
CATTLE, HORSES, SHEEP, PIGS,
AND ROOTS.

CHAIRMAN:
ALEXANDER F. LUTTRELL, ESQ.
The DINNER will be held in the LUTTRELL ARMS HOTEL, at 1.30.
Tickets to be had at the Hotel.

COMMITTEE:
Mr. R. CORNER, Torweston.
" W. L. CHORLEY, Quarme.
" T. NURCOMBE, Minehead.
" E. LOVELACE, Timberscombe.
" J. STRONG, Carhampton.
Mr. J. GATCHELL, Alcombe.
" J. JOYCE, Allercott.
" G. RISDON, Dunster.
" J. CLARKE, Hindon.
" T. H. RISDON, Washford.

HON. TREASURER:
Mr. J. LEVERSHA, Withycombe, Dunster.

HON. SECRETARY:
Mr. C. H. SAMSON, Dunster.

JUDGES OF HORSES AND STOCK:
COLONEL LUTTRELL, Badgworth Court.
Mr. J. TAZEWELL, Haygrove, Bridgwater.
Mr. J. LUTLEY, Hartswell, Wiveliscombe.
Mr. J. G. DAVIS, Blagroves, Milverton.

JUDGES OF ROOTS:
Mr. J. JOYCE. | Mr. GEO. RISDON. | Mr. T. LEVERSHA.

Price Threepence.

WILLITON:
S. COX, PRINTER, BOOKSELLER, STATIONER, &c., "FREE PRESS" OFFICE.

As early as 1800 there seems to have been in existence a Dunster Agricultural Society promoting competition between farmers and local breeders. A small silver cup still exists bearing the inscription, 'From the Dunster Agricultural Society to J.F. Luttrell, Esq., for the best store heifer having had a calf, not exceeding the age of 4 years. 1800.'

In 1835 an annual Christmas stock show and sale – the Great Christmas Market – was established. Each year at the end of November the old market-place was filled with sheep and cattle brought in to be sold at auction. A small 'exhibition of livestock' held in conjunction with the Christmas show and market was begun by Thomas Oatway of Priory Farm. The old farmhouse, which incorporated part of the former priory buildings, is situated beside the church, and the farm buildings and yards once covered all the area in front of the house and church, adjacent to the tithe barn and dovecot. This 'exhibition of livestock' was the origin of Dunster Show and Priory Farm is where the early shows were held for more than 30 years.

The first chairman of Dunster Show was Lieut. Col Francis Fownes Luttrell of Kilve, veteran of the Peninsular War and of Waterloo, chairman of Somerset Quarter Sessions, first chairman of the Williton Board of Guardians and for 32 years Master of the West Somerset Foxhounds which he founded – clearly a redoubtable figure. The Revd John King, vicar of Cutcombe, was another founder of the show. Those were the days when the clergy farmed their glebe land and Mr King liked to describe himself as 'a horn mutton farmer'. He was remembered as a particularly popular speaker at the luncheons that were held at the Luttrell Arms on each show day. Another clergyman who, a little later, was a regular supporter of the show was the vicar of Minehead, the Revd A.H.F. Luttrell, who gained a reputation for 'mangold wurzel' growing as, year after year, he was awarded first prize for the best half acre of roots.

The year 1860 saw the silver jubilee of the show. That year there were 22 classes which included 'pair of fat oxen, pair of fat steers, best cow or heifer, best bull, breeding cow in calf, calf heifer under two years'. There were three classes for

Priory Farm, c.1865–75

These pictures of Priory Farm were taken by James Date and repay detailed study. The top and centre pictures were taken in c.1865 before the old vicarage was built and show barns and walls that have since been pulled down. The tithe map of 1843 indicates that the dovecot (not shown) stood in the middle of a group of farm buildings and must be just to the right of the thatched building which may have been cowsheds and sited where the terraced garden is today. There seems to have been a sawpit in front of the thatched barn. The picture below was taken later, after 1872.

Christmas Fatstock Show, c.1907.

sheep and rams, two for pigs, four for horses and three for roots. The jumping competitions, which were later to become so popular, seem to have started a few years later.

In 1862 the decision was taken to charge 6d. for admission to the show which that year raised £5. By then the show was attracting breeders of top quality Red Devon cattle, some of which went on to win prizes at the Royal Agricultural Meeting and at Smithfield Club Show. The value of prize money had increased tremendously and in 1863 Dunster Great Market was described by a speaker at the dinner as having become a 'depot for beef to be consumed in the Metropolis'.

Three years later, in 1865, an epidemic of rinderpest or cattle plague swept the country, attacking up to 3,000 head of cattle a week, most of which never recovered. The disease had not yet reached the South West and at the show that year, 'the number and the quality of the stock exceeded that of any previous year'. Severe restrictions on horned cattle stopped the show in the two following years.

Dunster Show Officials, 1910. Standing: *Messrs A. Cuthill, Supt Perry, S.J. Partridge, H.W. Tomkins, W.J. Leversha, W.G. Thorne and A. Hole;* sitting: *Messrs J. Tudball, Jas. Ridler, T.H. Leversha, W. Tarr, F. Adams and F.S. Merson.*

By 1865 the site of the show, the Great Market and the Root Fair had been moved to Waglands, the fields between the Ball and Conygar Hill, where a travelling fair proved an additional attraction.

It hasn't been possible to identify these marquees on Dunster Lawns, photographed before 1880. They may be connected with the Horticultural Show, Cricket Week, or with military parades.

Cattle and sheep were still penned in the High Street.

From 1875 to 1886 monthly cattle auctions were held in the market-place, special market trains being advertised with cheap fares available to bring customers to Dunster. After 1886 these monthly sales were held in Williton, but the Great Cattle Market continued in Dunster High Street on the first Friday of each December until 1925.

By this time townsfolk were beginning to take a pride in their well-kept town and it is not surprising that on more than one occasion people wrote to the auctioneers, Messrs Hawkes and Risdon, to complain of the condition of the streets after the cattle had been penned there. During the 1890s it was decided that in future the show should be held in summer:

It was felt that there were great risks in bringing animals from comfortable pens and stalls and exhibiting them in the first week in December without any more than a hedge for shelter.

In September 1897, the show was held for the first time on Dunster Castle Lawns where it has been held regularly ever since, save during the war years and in 2001 when the foot and mouth epidemic prevented all agricultural shows.

Example and education fostered Victorian attitudes of thrift, self-sufficiency, unquestioning obedience and loyalty. Dunster Penny Bank encouraged weekly savings. The Dunster and Williton Agricultural Society, founded in 1838, was designed to develop agricultural skills such as ploughing and bee-keeping and rewarded those who had been in service longest with one master and those who had brought up most children without recourse to parish help.

In its first year, on 1 June, a sheep-shearing contest was held in the Home Farm Yard at Dunster Castle. Each man had to shear three sheep held in pens and chosen by lot. Two-and-a-half hours were allowed for catching and shearing the sheep and tying up the fleece while each competitor was allowed half a pint of ale for each sheep sheared and a shilling's worth of refreshments. Ploughing matches were held in alternate years at Williton and Dunster.

In the early part of the century Dunster had six or seven inns but the numbers dwindled. Some, including the George and the Horse and Crook, were turned into living accommodation though sometimes by a circuitous route which reflected the worthy aim of encouraging sobriety and even abstinence alongside profit, as we shall see. In 1879, Joseph Neades, the landlord of the Horse and Crook, was exhorted 'to extend custom but not encourage or permit drunkenness'. His successor, Henry Manning, died in 1901 and Mr Luttrell considered selling the property to the People's Refreshment House Association. Their rules stated that:

... intoxicants are not to be exposed with a view to attract customers but every means is to be taken on the other hand to expose food and non-alcoholic drinks so as to encourage their consumption.

The Horse and Crook, c.1900.

Formerly the George Inn in the High Street.

Left: *The Oak Room at the Luttrell Arms, c.1910.*

Above: *Dunster, c.1912.*

Right: *William Clitsome (1817–96) stands in the doorway of 5 The Ball (c.1880) behind his four sons: Robert; twins William and Alexander; and John. At one time their father was a gardener at Dunster Castle.*

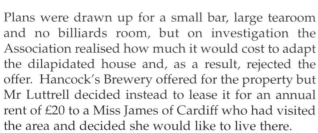

Plans were drawn up for a small bar, large tearoom and no billiards room, but on investigation the Association realised how much it would cost to adapt the dilapidated house and, as a result, rejected the offer. Hancock's Brewery offered for the property but Mr Luttrell decided instead to lease it for an annual rent of £20 to a Miss James of Cardiff who had visited the area and decided she would like to live there.

Miss James was one of a new class of resident who began to lease properties in Dunster round about 1900. Some had private incomes; others were members of the professions.

Throughout the 1800s visitors to Dunster stayed at the Luttrell Arms Hotel remarking on its hospitality and visiting the church, castle and grounds.

As the boom years ended and the population once again declined, the number of visitors increased and townsfolk began to turn their attention to providing meals and accommodation for them. A cyclist visiting Dunster in 1894 stopped at a cottage 'the mistress of which is willing to supply a simple meal, such as tea, new laid eggs, preserves, etc. for not more than three or four persons at a time.' Four years earlier J.Ll.W. Page wrote:

> *Dunster is one of the few, the very few, thoroughly old-fashioned country towns, in this utilitarian nineteenth century, spared to us. Whether we look down upon it from the crest of Grabhurst, the grounds of the castle or from either end of its main street, the same appearance of almost medieval aspect is presented, the same restful air broods over it. Here are no hideous modern villas, glaring with stucco. In their stead quaint thatched or tiled houses, one or two rich with ancient woodwork under peaked gables, blink in the sunshine at the curious wayfarer.*

At Home

Below: *Outside 30 West Street c.1905, the Sully family home until recently.* Left to right: *Arthur, Mrs Sully, Charles, Mrs Harrison (Mrs Sully's mother), Edward. At the back is Het Sully, big sister of the boys. Charles Sully was grandfather to Sylvia Sully (now Parsons).*

St George's Street, 1905. Some of these people may be members of the Griffiths' family.

Dunster Marsh, now Walnut Tree Cottage. There were several walnut trees nearby.

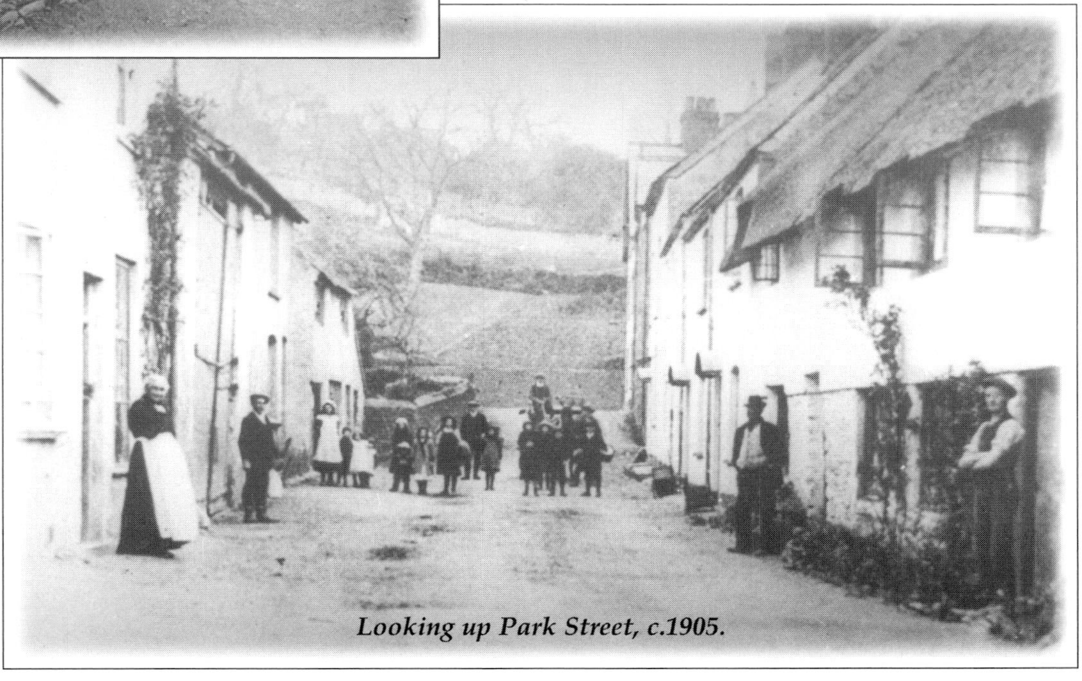

Looking up Park Street, c.1905.

Hunting

Over the years hunting has attracted many visitors to Dunster both as participants and onlookers.

Chapter Six

FAMILIES AT THE CASTLE

A fairytale castle.

Dunster Castle has been in the ownership of only two families, the de Mohuns and the Luttrells, from the time it was first built until very recently.

William de Mohun built the first castle soon after 1066. The tor was levelled, scarped for the top 80 feet (25m) and a simple but strong fortress and defences put up, probably constructed of timber. In building the first Norman castles the priority was speed so that they could be used in enforcing the Norman conquest of England. Gradually (according to the mid-twelfth-century *Gesta Stephani*) the walls and buildings were replaced in stone to form:

> *... impregnable defences... inaccessible on the one side where it was washed by the tide and very strongly fortified on the other by towers and walls, by a rampart and outworks.*

Whether the tide reached the castle mound at this time is a matter of debate.

During the 70 years following 1066, the de Mohuns administered their estates in Normandy and England profitably and made generous gifts to churches and monasteries in both countries. Gradually the de Mohuns acquired more property in England and in 1204 when Normandy was separated from England, Reynold de Mohun chose to pay homage to King John since his chief estates were now English. Reynold de Mohun II (died c.1213) built a new gatehouse at the castle (known today as the Gateway) and buildings for his own use in the lower ward of the castle. The great medieval walls can still be identified in the present castle. An extent or survey of 1266 identified the buildings still in use on the tor: a hall with buttery, pantry, kitchen and bake-house, a fair chapel, a knights' hall, three towers and a prison. The lower ward included three 'towers' or groups of buildings, and a granary. The cow-house,

The Gatehouse

Sir Hugh Luttrell's gatehouse built c.1420, photographed in c.1870 during the alterations to the castle. On the right of the picture on the left can be seen a railed track used for transporting building materials up the steep to the castle.

stable, dovecot and dairy lay below, near the river.

Over the next hundred years the de Mohuns proved powerful supporters of the Crown, fighting in wars in France, Wales and Scotland, and dutifully accepting the irksome burden of attending Parliament. Many of the de Mohuns died young and the Crown frequently benefited from their estates being held in wardship.

John de Mohun V (c.1320–75) inherited the estates when he was only ten years old and when he came of age married Joan de Burghersh, daughter of his first guardian. John was a brilliant soldier. He fought at Crecy alongside Edward, Prince of Wales, in the division said to comprise 'all the flower of the chivalry of England'. The prince later presented him with a fine charger, Grisel Gris. John was one of the original 25 Knights of the Garter but, like many professional soldiers, he found it hard to settle at home. As a young man he was involved in various felonies in Somerset, imprisoned and only released after royal intervention. He moved in wealthy circles and lived extravagantly, well beyond his means. At home he seems to have been under the thumb of his wife, Joan, while his three daughters, who all made sparkling marriages, must have added to his mounting debts. As the likelihood of there being a male heir diminished, Joan seems to have decided to look to her own future. A series of complex and legally suspect transactions gave her a life interest in her husband's estates and the right to dispose of the Dunster properties. In 1374, even before her husband's death, she set in motion the sale of the reversion of the Dunster estates to Lady Elizabeth Luttrell for 10,000 marks, a transaction completed in 1376. When John died, Joan shut up the castle and moved to be nearer the Court and the heart of the social scene, which she much preferred to country life. She lived for a while in London and in Canterbury where she died and was buried in an ornate tomb in the cathedral. She outlived the Lady Elizabeth.

The Luttrell family probably originated in France, for their name comes from 'loutre' meaning an otter. Geoffrey Luttrell (died c.1216) from Nottinghamshire was a supporter of King John and a trusted courier who frequently crossed to France on royal business. It was he who laid the foundation of the family fortunes by marrying the heiress Frethesant Paynell (Paganel). Their son, Andrew, inherited his grandfather's Paynell estates and successfully laid claim on the death of a third cousin, Maurice of Gaunt, to several manors in Lincolnshire and Somerset, including East Quantoxhead. This was always a favourite residence which still belongs to the Luttrell family.

Lady Elizabeth Luttrell who bought the reversion was a great lady in her own right: a granddaughter of Edward I, sister to the Archbishop of Canterbury and the widow of Sir John de Vere, son of the Earl of Oxford. She married, doubtless for love, into a junior branch of the Luttrell family and it was her son Hugh (c.1364–1428) who, on the death of Joan de Mohun and aware that the Dunster inheritance arrangements might be challenged, acted quickly to establish his claim. In spite of moves by the de Mohun daughters and their influential husbands,

Hugh was able to establish the upper hand and by 1406 could feel sure of his inheritance. By then he had ousted the tenants from the castle and moved in with his wife and household to celebrate Christmas 1405. Clean rushes were strewn on Christmas Eve; they feasted on venison, capons and pork and were entertained with music and dancing performed by the townsfolk and children of Dunster and Minehead. It may well have been very cold in the castle for the Luttrell ladies ordered fur for their gowns and Hugh soon had glass installed in the windows.

Hugh Luttrell was a man of wealth and influence, the personal and trusted envoy of both Richard II and Henry IV. He fought in Wales against Owain Glendower and in France; he eventually became Lieutenant of Harfleur and Seneschal of Normandy, representing the English interest. Surviving accounts show that he and his family lived at the castle in style, surrounded by a retinue of servants dressed in colourful liveries with embroidered pockets. Meat, game and fish were bought for the lord's table, the latter often secured live and kept till needed in the fish-ponds in the Hangar Park. There were purchases, too, of imported luxuries; ginger and pepper, olive oil, almonds, dates, figs and raisins. Hugh restored the neglected fabric of the castle, securing doors, refurnishing the kitchens and making all water-tight with Mendip lead. In 1420 the new gatehouse was begun, which still stands. With its six smallish rooms, each with a fire-place, it must have been a comfortable addition to the older rambling buildings.

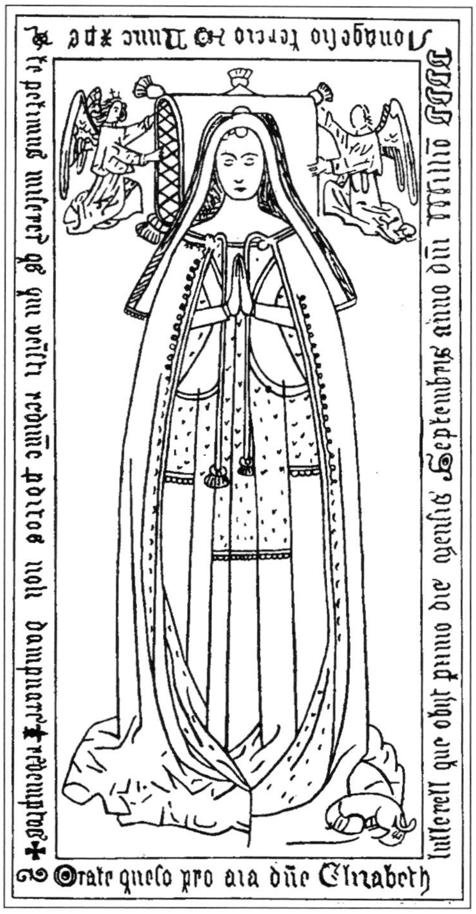

Dame Elizabeth (Courtenay of Powderham), widow of James Luttrell who died from wounds received at the second battle of St Albans.

During the following century little was done to the castle. Hugh's heir died within two years of his father and the inheritance passed to his four-year-old son. Then in 1455 civil war broke out between the Yorkists and Lancastrians, rival claimants to the throne. James Luttrell, a strong Lancastrian supporter, went north to join the army of Henry VI. He was knighted on the battlefield of Wakefield but seven weeks later was wounded at St Albans and died soon after. As the Yorkists seized power, James Luttrell and fellow Lancastrians were charged with high treason and the Dunster estates declared forfeit and given to the King's favourite, William Herbert. James' widow, Elizabeth, was left homeless but soon remarried and was able to repossess some of her inheritance. The remainder of the property was not recovered until the death of Richard III. Even then the castle was not lived in very much; Hugh (d.1521) preferred East Quantoxhead, John (c.1519–51) was away in the wars and Thomas (1525–71) lived at Marshwood. Only Andrew (d.1538) lived in the castle for a while and almost certainly found it cold, inconvenient and old-fashioned.

George Luttrell (1560–1629) was to change that. He inherited at the age of 11, became a Fellow Commoner at Caius College, Cambridge and was admitted as a member of Gray's Inn. He acquired a reputation for enjoying legal squabbles and being a 'builder'. He married twice, both times to ladies disapproved of by his family. Joan, the daughter of his lawyer guardian, Hugh Stewkley, often at odds with the Luttrells, was described as 'a slutte' who had no good qualities while the termagant Sylvestra Capps, his second wife, was 'an obscure person from Wiveliscombe'. East Quantoxhead was part of her marriage portion and she lived there with subsequent husbands who suffered, along with the servants, from 'her wicked ways'. Her second husband in his will left 20s. 'to Giles Baker, my servant who hath lived under the tyranny of my wife, to the danger of his life, during the space of two years.'

George was responsible for building a new harbour in Minehead and the Yarn Market in Dunster, for redesigning what is now the Luttrell Arms Hotel and altering substantially the family homes at East Quantoxhead and Marshwood. He went on to convert the medieval jumble of buildings in the lower ward of the castle into a Jacobean mansion, quarrelling with his architect William Arnold over the cost and quality of the work. As we have seen, the new house within the medieval defences withstood attack during the Civil War. However, at the end of the war, because the Luttrells had for a time supported the Royalist cause, an order went out for the castle to be demolished and in 1650 a gang of a hundred men was sent in. They totally razed the buildings on the tor, the towers and most of the curtain wall but a last-minute order countermanding the first was just in time to save the dwelling-house and Hugh Luttrell's gatehouse.

During the Civil War, a political pamphleteer, William Prynne, was imprisoned in the castle for protesting against the execution of Charles I and denouncing the Parliamentary regime. For his earlier supposed attacks on the King and Queen and on the bishops, he had lost both ears and had been branded on the cheeks, 'SL', seditious libeller. He was only allowed to speak with others in the presence of his gaoler but seems to have been given free run of the castle and spent his time usefully calendaring the 'confused chaos' of the Luttrell muniments. Prynne's work forms the basis of the catalogue of the comprehensive collection of Luttrell archives held today in the Somerset Record Office.

Little was done to dispel the gloom of military occupation at the castle until 1680 when Francis Luttrell married the beautiful heiress, Mary Tregonwell of Milton Abbas in Dorset. They adopted a fashionable and sumptuous lifestyle. Hundreds of pounds were spent on clothes for themselves and their children. Francis' uniforms were, according to his tailor, made of cloth 'much better than the other officers' and the male servants were arrayed in liveries with gorgeous trimmings of black and gold lace. The castle was altered to provide a fitting setting for this extravagance and the ornate plaster ceilings and elaborately carved staircase depicting stag and fox hunting scenes were installed at this time.

Francis led the local militia at the time of Monmouth's Rebellion and in 1688 raised a troop of foot in support of William of Orange. When the troop was incorporated into a regiment Francis Luttrell became its first colonel: the regiment was later to be known as the Green Howards. He died in 1690, only 31, and his widow took most of the furniture with her to her London house. Narcissus Luttrell wrote in his diary for 19 November 1696:

> *Yesterday morning a sudden fire hapned in Mrs Luttrell's house in St James's Street, being newly and richly furnished, which burnt it to the ground, the lady herself narrowly escaping and 'tis said she lost in plate, jewells, etc. to the value of £10,000.*

A few weeks later Mary Luttrell married the Swedish merchant, Jacob Bancks, who is said to have rescued her from the flames. She died of smallpox in 1704.

Not surprisingly, Francis Luttrell left debts which were still being paid off in 1720 by his brother Alexander's widow, Dorothy, who on her husband's death took up the management of the estates for her son. She had a reputation for kindliness and good sense and was responsible for building an ornate chapel at the back of the castle and a new and easier approach road, besides repairing Minehead's harbour.

Dorothy's granddaughter, Margaret, inherited the Dunster estates in 1737 when she was 11. She was to make a wise choice of husband in her second cousin, Henry Fownes of Nethway in South Devon, for their marriage was happy and he was prepared to spend his own money to set the rocky fortunes of the Luttrell family back on an even keel. His portrait shows him as a solid and sensible country squire and his sensitive landscaping of the castle and grounds

The Picturesque

The Palladian (Lawns) Bridge (above) *and Rustic Bridge* (left) *were built as part of Henry Fownes Luttrell's landscaping of the castle grounds.*

Left: *Henry Fownes Luttrell. From a drawing by Richard Phelps.*

Right: *George Fownes Luttrell.*

succeeded in enhancing his country way of life. The beautiful setting of the castle owes much to the vision of Henry Fownes Luttrell. He was interested in country pursuits – horses, hounds, and fighting cocks – and created an ornamental deer park to replace that at Marshwood, Carhampton. He levelled the tor and laid a bowling green and employed the artist Richard Phelps, much esteemed as a portrait painter by local families though described by Henry Maxwell-Lyte as 'rather indifferent', to design the romantic bridges, arches and waterfalls near the mill as well as Conygar Tower with its mock ruins now shrouded in trees. How grand it must have been to have a 'castle' at either end of the village!

The work on building the tower on Conygar Hill was carried out during the summer of 1775. Stone was quarried and foundations dug and then wooden scaffolding, tied with tarred rope, was raised as the masons worked on the tower. The stone was all wheeled in barrows to the site – 320 loads of lime were delivered; three men worked for 62½ days digging clay and a man or boy spent 52 days with horse and cart drawing water and clay to the site. As usual, cider was provided daily and when the job was finished there was 'entertainment' for the 15 men who had worked on the job. The archways and towers to the north of Conygar were completed soon after.

Edmund Rack, Collinson's collaborator on *The History and Antiquities of the County of Somerset* published in 1791, tells us more about the tower:

On the north side just across the town rises a noble steep hill called Conegar 300 feet high. Viewed from the east it has a conical form and is clothed with wood from top to bottom. On the highest point of the hill is a handsome tower 60 feet high, from the top of which is a finely diversified and extensive prospect. A winding circular road is cut from the bottom to the top of the hill and about half way up, on the side next the sea are some modern built ruins, well executed, which have a fine effect from the water. On a high pedestal near these ruins is placed a large statue of Neptune which may be distinctly seen from the sea. On each side [of] *this spiral ascent are several rustic seats which command the most picturesque and pleasing views.*

About 200 yards from the tower, in the thickest part of the wood stands a little thatched house, the roof of which is supported by the branches of trees whose trunks form its sides. The walls are composed of matted reeds, through which several branches of the trees are interwoven and enliven it with their verdure. It is finished with a cupboard, a table and seats and cold collations are sometimes served up here to company. The building consists of only one room which is open towards the sea; and not a vessel or boat can pass without being seen from it.

The parallels with the landscaping of the Acland estates at Holnicote and at Killerton in Devon and of Halswell at Goathurst near Bridgwater are remarkable.

Henry Fownes Luttrell took a rather reluctant interest in politics but nurtured the borough of Minehead so that it was largely back in the family pocket from 1768 until 1832 when it was disenfranchised by the Great Reform Act.

Henry's son John stood as Member of Parliament for Minehead and followed his father in managing the Dunster properties as a country estate but his sons John (1787–1857) and Henry (1790–1867) Fownes Luttrell were both unmarried and often away. The wife of a visitor to the castle in 1845 wrote of the fine views but mediocre and old-fashioned furniture. Elizabeth Ernst, visiting Dunster in the mid-nineteenth century, described 'a sad picture of departed greatness', the owner an inveterate bachelor, generally in London, while 'two old maiden aunts' lived in the castle in great seclusion. The stables and kennels were empty and the servants, with little to do, numbered 'twenty idle people'.

It is not surprising that very soon after George Fownes Luttrell inherited in 1867, he decided on a drastic reconstruction of the castle to make it a more comfortable place to live. He engaged the distinguished and experienced architect, Antony

Conygar Tower

Conygar Tower was built as a folly in 1775 and mock Roman arches were built nearby as part of Henry Fownes Luttrell's landscaping of the castle grounds.

Above: *Dunster Castle before the reconstruction began in 1867.*

The Gateway in the 1870s.

Above: *The curtain walls and gatehouse in the 1870s.*

Salvin, who, with sympathetic eye, remodelled the interior, adding two new towers and a service wing to the old Jacobean house and successfully medievalising the exterior. He aimed to make the castle look and feel as if it had been constantly restored and improved – as it had been – rather than rebuilding in the style of one specific period.

The work was begun in 1867 and completed by the end of 1872. In January 1873 neighbouring gentry and clergy were invited to a ball at the castle along with tenants who paid an annual rent of £50 or more. For most of the guests this would have been their first opportunity to view the impressive restoration. Seven years later the Prince of Wales paid a private two-day visit to the castle, primarily for the hunting. He travelled by train to Dunster Station where he was greeted by townsfolk who accompanied him to the castle between houses decorated with flowers and greenery.

The castle after its reconstruction by Antony Salvin in 1872.

The castle gardens had been well tended since the 1700s. In 1830 James Savage remarked on the famous lemon tree, intrigued by the ingenious moveable frame which protected it in winter. A tree was in existence as early as 1759 when sailcloth was ordered to cover 'the frames of the lemon tree'. During 1764–5, 50 plum trees and 40 quinces were planted alongside numerous apple trees. Over 80 glass frames for cucumbers and melons were purchased and a greenhouse heated by an oil-fired 'ingin' was repaired. The vegetable gardens were prolific, growing every imaginable vegetable including 'collyflowers', hotspur peas, garlick, shot top radishes and cardoons. Cottage flowers such as sweet peas and nasturtiums were grown in the walled gardens in contrast to the shrubs and exotica planted close to the castle itself. In later years limpet shells were ordered by the ton to be used as fertiliser.

The castle grounds were open to the public from the 1870s in aid of the Village Hospital. Arrangements and fees varied over the years but in 1871 there seems to have been a two-tier system for visitors. Tourists changing horses or staying

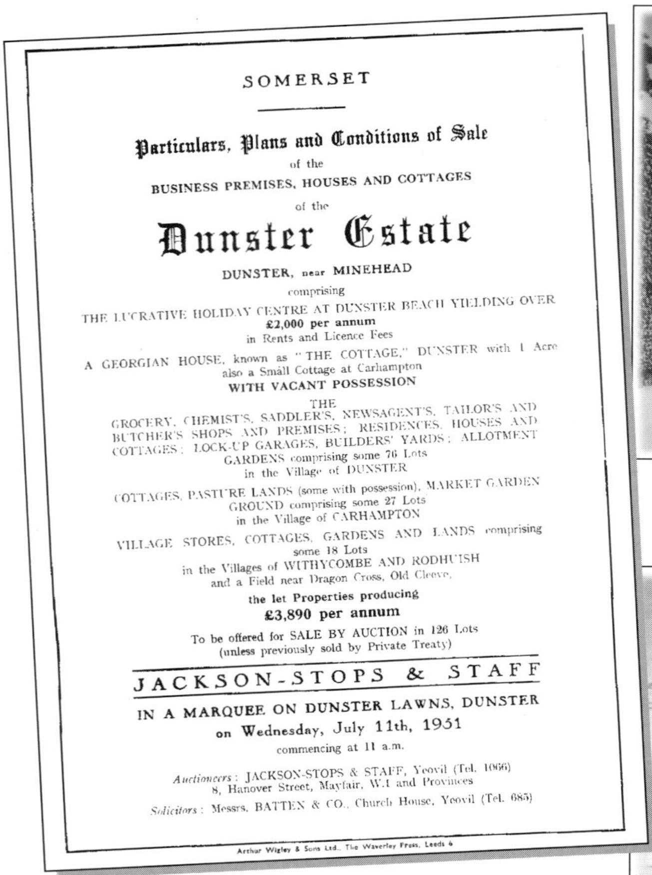

SOMERSET

Particulars, Plans and Conditions of Sale
of the
BUSINESS PREMISES, HOUSES AND COTTAGES
of the

Dunster Estate

DUNSTER, near MINEHEAD
comprising
THE LUCRATIVE HOLIDAY CENTRE AT DUNSTER BEACH YIELDING OVER
£2,000 per annum
in Rents and Licence Fees
A GEORGIAN HOUSE, known as "THE COTTAGE," DUNSTER with 1 Acre
also a Small Cottage at Carhampton
WITH VACANT POSSESSION
THE
GROCERY, CHEMIST'S, SADDLER'S, NEWSAGENT'S, TAILOR'S AND BUTCHER'S SHOPS AND PREMISES; RESIDENCES, HOUSES AND COTTAGES; LOCK-UP GARAGES, BUILDERS' YARDS; ALLOTMENT GARDENS comprising some 76 Lots
in the Village of DUNSTER
COTTAGES, PASTURE LANDS (some with possession), MARKET GARDEN GROUND comprising some 27 Lots
in the Village of CARHAMPTON
VILLAGE STORES, COTTAGES, GARDENS AND LANDS comprising some 18 Lots
in the Villages of WITHYCOMBE AND RODHUISH
and a Field near Dragon Cross, Old Cleeve,
the let Properties producing
£3,890 per annum
To be offered for SALE BY AUCTION in 126 Lots
(unless previously sold by Private Treaty)

JACKSON-STOPS & STAFF

IN A MARQUEE ON DUNSTER LAWNS, DUNSTER
on Wednesday, July 11th, 1951
commencing at 11 a.m.

Auctioneers: JACKSON-STOPS & STAFF, Yeovil (Tel. 1066)
8, Hanover Street, Mayfair, W.1 and Provinces
Solicitors: Messrs. BATTEN & CO., Church House, Yeovil (Tel. 685)

Arthur Wigley & Sons Ltd., The Waverley Press, Leeds 6

Above: *Staff at the castle, c.1890.*

Right: *Dunster Castle Gardens. On the left is Mr Webber, Head Gardener 1887–1900. He left to start Webber's Nurseries in Minehead. (Courtesy Mr J.J. Webber, his grandson.)*

overnight at the Luttrell Arms Hotel might buy a ticket to view the gardens at any time save on Sunday and could buy a family ticket for 2s.6d. if there were enough of them. However, respectable persons residing in the neighbourhood might only visit the gardens on Tuesday afternoons and had to pay full price for their cards of admission: 1s. for two people.

George Luttrell and his successors took their responsibilities to their tenants seriously and many of the improvements made in Minehead and Dunster were initiated and, in some part at least, paid for by the family. Their concern and generosity is more marked when we realise that there was little money to spare; the property and estates were most carefully managed and even the tiniest source of income, such as rabbiting or whortleberry picking, could not be ignored.

Alexander Fownes Luttrell, 1944.

When Alexander Luttrell died in 1944 he had not made over either castle or estate to his heirs. Crippling death duties were incurred and in 1949 Geoffrey Luttrell was forced to sell. The Ashdale Property Company bought the major part of the 8,600-acre Dunster estate in 1949 and this was later sold in 1954 to the Commissioners for Crown Lands. The castle and grounds passed to Colonel Walter Luttrell on the death of his father (1957) and he, when his mother died, gave the house, gardens and Old Park to the National Trust in 1976.

Chapter Seven

THE CHURCH & ITS PEOPLE

Dunster Church, c.1910.

At the western end of Dunster Church, set in the floor of the south aisle, is a brass memorial. Its Latin inscription commemorates John Wyther, baker, Agnes, his wife and their eldest son John, and it bears the date, the penultimate day of September 1487. Two solemn figures wearing the clothes of prosperous townspeople of the period are cut in the brass.

John and Agnes Wyther.

John Wyther, or his son, was one of a group of the principal men of Dunster who banded together early in the reign of Henry VII to establish the independence of the parish and deny the prior and monks of Dunster certain traditional fees, offerings and rights. The petition from the monks even states 'that to fulfil and satisfie theire croked appetites, thei toke up the bell roopis and said that the Priour and Convent there should have no bells there to ring.'

It is unlikely that John Wyther and his fellows – Thomas Upcott, merchaunt; Thomas Kodogon, yeoman; Adam Wilkyns, clothemaker; William Crasse, bocher; Symond Pers, yoman; John Greyme, yoman; John Philippis, tanner; John Paynter, barbour; John Morgan, parker; and Martyn Glover – saw the matter in this light. Dunster in the fifteenth century was a thriving market and woollen town. The burgesses and tradesmen were wealthy men, many managing their own businesses and travelling widely. Their Christian beliefs were deep-rooted but their independence and initiative led them to challenge the rights of the small group of monks, bound by rules and tradition, who dominated their church life and worship. They wanted more say in the governing of their church and to spend some part of their profits to the greater glory of God, by rebuilding the church as did their contemporaries in Gloucestershire and Suffolk. The origins of this dispute and others, which developed in the 1400s, can be found in the earlier history of the church in Dunster.

Nothing is known of Christianity in Dunster before about 1100. About 500 years earlier the people of the area were listening to the preaching of missionaries such as Carantoc, Decuman and Keyna who had crossed from Wales and found places to live near the coast. Their dynamic words and lives were responsible for the conversion of many; churches were dedicated in their honour and legends grew around their memory. The steps and stump of a cross in the churchyard at Dunster mark the place where preachers set up wooden crosses and spoke to the gathered crowds about Christ long before even the simplest church was built in the parish.

Some time during the last decade of the eleventh century, the first William de Mohun gave the church of St George at Dunster together with land at Alcombe, the tithes of several manors and two fisheries, one at Dunster and one at Carhampton, to the Benedictine abbey at Bath. Although by that time there was probably a small church in the town these gifts were for the purpose of 'building and raising' the church, a task which was completed during the next century. The solid Norman work can still be seen in the west and north walls of the nave.

The Norman church was just over 80 feet (24m) long and nearly 25 feet (8m) wide, with a fairly flat wooden roof and a large round-headed arch leading to the chancel. There may have been a low tower. The monks from Bath Abbey responsible for building the church would have lived in basic accommodation while the important work of raising a church for the worship of God was being carried out. Once it was complete they would have been able to turn their attention to building something more permanent around the cloister set beside the northern wall of the church. The priory is first mentioned in 1177 and, by the reign of King John (1199–1216), was well established and able to provide accommodation, food and stabling for the vicar of Dunster, Richard the Chaplain, who was not one of the monks but responsible for the needs and worship of the parish.

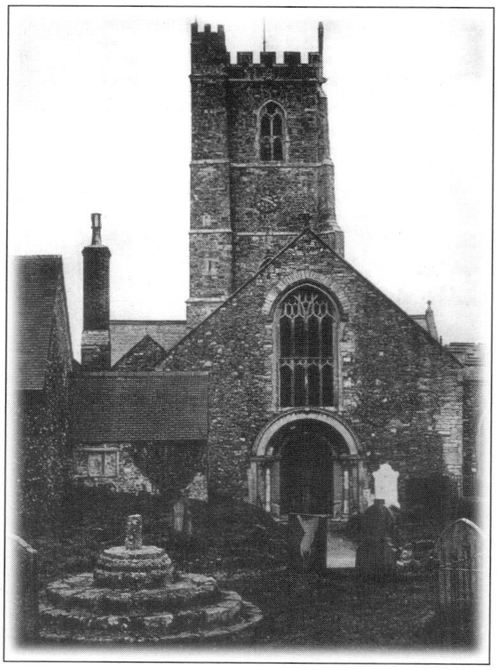

The steps and stump are all that remain of Dunster's medieval preaching cross.

During the reign of Henry III (1216–72), the choir of the church was enlarged (now the much restored east end), and people gave generously to found and maintain chantries such as the chapel of St Lawrence, mentioned first in 1254, where prayers were said constantly for the souls of the departed.

From 1262 the priory had a more distinct organisation. Its endowments were increased by the de Mohun family and the monks held and farmed a separate manor, a fair-sized area of land to the north of the church and in Alcombe where they also served a small chapel. In the south aisle can be seen the inscribed tombstone of Adam of Cheddar, prior c.1338–55, who was responsible for 'sumptuous buildings' that may have included the priory itself. At one point the dorter where the monks slept was close to the north wall and no doubt the usual night stair led directly into the church so that the monks were able to reach the chancel for the night services without venturing outside. A penthouse roof would have covered a walkway around the cloister garth where monks would have written at raised desks similar to the one with the sloping lid now used in the church as a chest. The present buildings known as the Old Priory were built in the later fifteenth century and housed the prior's lodgings together with kitchens and storerooms. Legacies and other gifts to the priory were doubtless generous – take, for example, the 28s.6d. left to the priory by Richard Bruton, once vicar of Minehead.

In 1357 the difficulties of sharing a church building between monks and the parish began to emerge. An agreement was made between the prior, Richard of Childeston, the monks and the parishioners. On Sundays they were to unite in one procession and together attend the conventual High Mass at the altar of St George in the chancel where the parishioners would make their offerings four times a year. At Mass the parishioners would stand in the nave and it is easy to imagine that they would feel dissatisfied and cut off from the worship led at the far end of the church and separated from them by screens. Other clauses of the agreement referred to the provision of candles, expensive at the time, and the division of responsibilities regarding the upkeep of the building.

In 1420, William Pynsoun, 'citizen of Dunster', bequeathed 6s.8d. to the work on the new rood-loft, 40s. to the building of the new bell tower and 20s. for a new bell. This work was evidently begun soon after, for in 1443 a contract was drawn up between the churchwardens and John Marys, a builder of Stoke Courcy, who was to finish the bell tower by adding two further stages to the work already begun. The tower above the 'grass-tabyl' was to be 100 feet (30m) high; it was to have three French buttresses and a 'vice' or staircase in the fourth corner. Four windows in the belfry were each to have two lights separated by a 'moynell' and divided by a 'trawnsom' designed by Richard Pope, freemason. The main walls were to be 4 feet (1.25m) thick up to the 'bell-bed' and 3 feet 6 inches (1m) above. There was to be a 'batylment', three 'gargylles' and four 'pynacles'. The parish would provide materials and equipment and Marys was to receive 13s.4d. for 'workemanchyppe' and 20s. extra for carving the pinnacles. Once the tower was complete a rood-loft was set up between the western arches of the tower. The doorway leading to it from the new tower staircase can still be seen. It supported the altar of the Holy Cross that was used regularly in parish worship. Another screen with doors leading to the chancel crossed between the eastern arches. A new roof, almost flat, with carved bosses and massive ribs, was placed over the Norman nave and both monks and parishioners contributed to work in the north and south transepts.

Soon after this, trouble blew up again between priory and parish and in 1498 matters were taken to arbitration in Glastonbury and an agreement reached which effectively divided the church into two parts. The monks were to occupy the east end and the vicar and parish the west where they were to 'build and maintain' a new and separate choir, though this was not to supersede the high altar at the east end.

An immediate result was the construction of the wonderful carved rood-screen that crosses the whole breadth of the church two bays west of the tower. This section became the new parochial chancel. But before this could be completed the nave had to be reconstructed, the south aisle enlarged and the nave roof replaced by the present wagon roof. The earlier roof seems to have been adapted to cover the south aisle. The north aisle was rebuilt soon after 1504 when Thomas Upcot left ten tons of iron 'to the new aisle there to be built or repaired on the north side.' The west window was installed in about 1530 together with the octagonal font, its delicate carving depicting the five wounds of Christ and the instruments of the Passion.

The dual use of the church established in 1498 did not last long for in 1539 Dunster Priory was dissolved and John Leland, visiting Dunster soon after 1540, wrote: 'The hole church of the late priory servith now for the paroche church. Aforetymes the monks had the est part closed up to their use.' The priory buildings and lands passed into the hands of the crown and were at first leased by John Luttrell (uncle of young John Luttrell who had recently inherited the castle) who lived in what was later to be known as Priory Farm beside the church. In 1543 the property was sold but bought through an agent by John Luttrell's sister-in-law and remained in Luttrell hands. The rectory, the tithe receipts and the responsibility for appointing a vicar, was also leased by John Luttrell at first but was soon conveyed through various hands to Hugh Stewkley who in 1566 was accused of not making proper provision for a curate although he was receiving the tithe income. (The lack of provision for a priest was always a problem in the parish, there being only a minimal endowment to support a clergyman until 1872 when a new vicarage was built and the cure properly endowed.)

The rood-screen.

Eventually these responsibilities passed to the Luttrells and by 1643 the chancel was no longer used for parish worship but had become a place of burial for the family who had their private chapel at the castle. It is conceivable that the parishioners preferred the spacious nave to the old priory church, which was rapidly becoming dilapidated. As late as 1703 timber and tiles were being taken from the 'cloister court', some being sold for building purposes, some used for church repairs but all regarded as the property of the parish. It seems that there was never a clear distinction between what belonged to the parish and what belonged to the castle.

However neglected the church building was at the end of the seventeenth century, there was always plenty of money to be spent by the parish on the bells that were rung to mark occasions such as the death of William of Orange's queen, Mary, the coronation of George I and the peace of Utrecht – all to the accompaniment of gallons of beer. Ropes and clappers often had to be replaced but in 1684 one of the bells was recast in a furnace somewhere between Loxhole and Conygar and maybe near the pottery kiln behind the Luttrell Arms Hotel where there was a building named the Bell House, which is shown on the Tithe Map of 1843. Later bells were carted to Watchet or Minehead and then shipped to Bristol for recasting.

In 1717 a gallery was put up at the west of the nave to accommodate musicians and singers, and in 1728 £40 was paid to Richard Phelps, the Porlock artist and Luttrell protégée, for restoring the altarpiece.

A period of neglect followed, which reflects the downturn in the town's fortunes. Both Collinson in 1791 and Savage in 1830 spoke of the dilapidated state of the church and particularly the chancel. Collinson reported that the priory church – the east end once used by the monks for their daily offices – was in a poor state of repair. It was

The Articles of Ringing

I *You that in Ringing take delight*
Be pleased to draw Near
These Articles you must observe
If you mean to ring here.

II *And first if any Overturn*
A Bell as that he may
He forthwith for that only Fault
In Beer shall sixpence pay.

III *If any one shall Curse or Swear*
When he come within the door
He then shall Forfeit for that Fault
As mentioned before.

IV *If anyone shall wear his Hat*
When he is ringing here
He straightway then shall sixpence pay
In Cyder or in Beer.

V *If anyone these Articles*
Refuseth to Obey
Let him have nine Stripes of ye Rope
And to depart Away.

William Gale, John Withers
Churchwardens 177(1)

The rood-screen and east window (c.1500) before restoration. Box pews fill the nave and to the right is the three-decker pulpit crowned with sounding board.

Left: *William Long (1819–84) was Parish Clerk from 1861 until his death. In 1885 his son John was appointed Clerk in his place.*

Right: *On Sunday 18 October 1874 the church collections were given to the Parish Church Restoration Fund. They amounted to £6.4s.8d. which included four gold sovereigns together with 94 silver and 123 copper coins.*

no better when James Savage was writing. In 1830 it was being used mainly as a dumping ground for rubbish. Rough stone walls divided it from the rest of the church and the ancient screen in the south aisle had been whitewashed.

The Parish Church was filled with huge wooden box pews and the west end blocked off by the singing gallery installed in 1717 at a cost of £24.4s.7d. and £2.3s.7d. for beer for the workmen. At the front was a three-decker pulpit. In 1838 the architect S.C. Buckler surveyed the building and in cryptic language condemned the church as ruinous, damp, draughty and dangerous. The nave was filled with a hotchpotch of box pews, 'the most promiscuous, unseemly and uncomfortable assemblage of pews that can be met with' and it seems, too, that the odour in Dunster Church may not always have been that of sanctity. Unbelievable though it may seem, it was common practice for families who held pews in the church to bury their dead beneath the floors of these pews in shallow brick graves. When opened the graves were often found to be deep in black, fetid water with the coffins floating or overturned. It is little wonder that the worship of the time had little dignity.

Prebendary Hancock, vicar of Dunster in 1905, recounted stories told to him by older parishioners of the unseemly behaviour of lads in the gallery, where young boys and farm labourers sat as well as the singers. The sexton walked up and down between the seats to keep order and, on occasion, suspecting misbehaviour, would climb the winding gallery stairs by which time, of course, all would be still and silent. Nonetheless, allowing no benefit of doubt, he would rap some screeching boy on the head with his stave of office. The Clerk, William Long, was seated in the stall below the pulpit, and would announce each metrical psalm in sonorous tones, then mount the gallery to take up his bass viol alongside the two fiddles, flute and violoncello that accompanied the choir in complex contrapuntal hymns and psalms. Once the singing was over he would return to his stall before the service could proceed.

This gloomy state of affairs together with the economic problems of the people, provided fertile ground for the Methodist evangelists. Rowland Hill preached in Dunster in 1771 and by 1809 a Methodist meeting had been established in the town. In 1811 premises in Mill Lane were purchased and a chapel built. The meeting flourished and in 1832 a plot of land on the corner of West Street and St George's Street was bought. The shops and unfinished cottages on the site were incorporated into a new chapel and for some years the cause thrived, encouraged by the conversion of Mrs Langdon, the personal maid of the two Miss Luttrells at the castle. With the revival of fortunes in the town and the generous interest of Mr George Luttrell in the church and school, Methodism lost ground. The chapel had to be rebuilt in 1878 but soon after that the Wesleyan day school closed and only a small, but loyal membership remained during the twentieth century. The chapel finally closed in 1968.

Following Buckler's highly critical report, a minimal amount of repair work was carried out in the church including the installation of a Bryson organ in the west gallery which replaced the instruments and choir whose music was now considered vulgar and rubbishy by church reformers. Then, in 1875, a complete restoration was begun under the sensitive guidance of the architect G.E. Street ably assisted by G.H. Samson who saw the work through. These days the restoration might have been done differently but as Dr Francis Eeles wrote: 'Very great care was taken of every detail and Mr Street's new fittings are marked by dignity and restraint.' A large Perpendicular window at the east end of the church was removed and replaced by three thirteenth-century-style lancet windows constructed from

The Six O'Clock Bell

Charlie Thrush ringing the six o'clock bell. Now known as the Angelus Bell, it has until recently been rung morning and night for 300 years or more to mark the beginning and end of the working day.

remains found in the vicinity of the church by Mr Samson. The west doorway was enlarged and new choir stalls, enclosed by screens, were put up in what was to be known as the priory church. The gallery and box pews were removed and a new high altar was set up under the central tower a little to the east. Part of the screen that once crossed between the eastern arches of the tower was moved to the curiously shaped thirteenth-century arch in the south transept, which had been widened in either the fifteenth or sixteenth century. The Bryson organ was moved to the north aisle where it was powered by a complicated hydraulic system. When this eventually failed, a hand pump was installed.

The medieval altar stone in the priory church was discovered placed upside down in an aisle when electrical cables were being laid. It has been restored to its rightful position. Whether it had been overturned for safe keeping during the Puritan occupation of Dunster when it is said that the church was used as accommodation by the soldiers, or cast on one side when altars were ordered to be replaced by communion tables in 1550, we shall probably never know.

Since the restoration, Dunster Church has been well cared for by both the clergy and the people of Dunster. They were encouraged particularly by Dr Francis Eeles who wrote an excellent church guide and, from September 1939 until his death in 1954, ran the Council for the Care and Preservation of Churches from Earlham, his home in St George's Street, Dunster.

Dunster Bells

Above: *Arthur Tudball at receipt of custom at an exhibition in the Memorial Hall to raise money for the recasting of the bells.*

Top right: *Harry Lloyd* (left), *with his little dog, inspects the bells.*

Right: *Jack and Arthur Tudball take a closer look.*

Dunster Bells

Left: *The empty bell frame.*

Below: *Dunster Church bells on their way to be recast, 1968. Harry Lloyd* (left), *Aubrey Gould* (centre) *and Barry Rogers* (back right) *assist the bell hangers.*

Right: *The bell hangers from Taylors of Loughborough remove the bells.*

Dunster Bells

Jack Tudball (churchwarden) and Arthur Tudball (tower steward).

Dunster Choir

Right: *The Choir, c.1935.* Left to right, back row: *Philip Buckland, Gordon Griffiths, Michael Case, Bill Greenslade, Jack Rowe;* third row: *Fred Heard, George Maidment, Karl Meddick, Arthur Tudball, Jack Haydon, Tom Elliott, Tom Tudball, F. Buckland, Mr Day;* included in the second row are: *Olive Long, Eva Simpson, Philip Rowe, Maurice Case, Wesley Gould, Jack Herod, Mrs Day, Mrs Hopwood;* front row: *Peter Tudball, Miss Harris, Ira Gould, Norman Case, Prebendary Burney, Mr Amherst (organist), Fred Furse, Cecil Davis, Miss Yates, Percy Veale.*

Right: *Dunster schoolchildren visit the church to rehearse their nativity play, c.1975.*

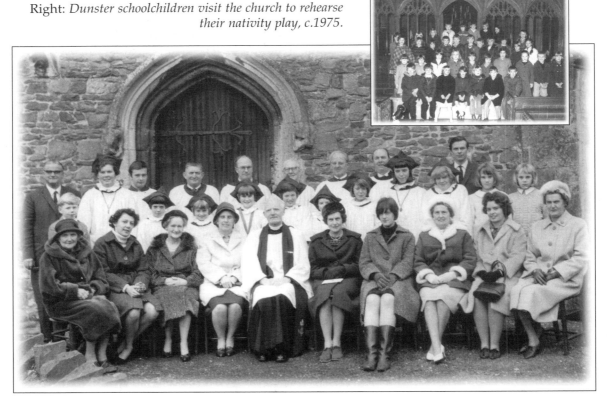

Dunster Choir at the Revd M. McCormick's last service. Left to right, back row: *Harold Langdon (choir master), Ann Bennett, John Dainton, Karl Meddick, Bill Dainton, Horace Arscott, Bob Burford, John Prowles, David Oliver (organist);* centre: *Steven Sanford, Avril Webber, ?, Janice Tudball, Julia Case, Vera Martin, Judith Hobbs, Christine Martin, Christine Case, Linda Sanford, Lorraine Sanford;* front: *Mrs Ratcliffe, Pauline Hawkins, Mrs Batchelor, Olive Dainton, Mr McCormick, Mrs McCormick, Phyllida McCormick, Violet Meddick, Ann Dainton, Alice Haydon.*

Chapter Eight

A Walk Around St George's Church

Church Street, c.1910. The bay windows on the right were removed, c.1938. On the left is the Priest's House, now much restored. In spite of rationing scrumptious teas were available here during the 1940s. Everyone sat around a large table covered with a white cloth and helped themselves to fresh bread, fruit cake, jam and cream.

It is best to begin a visit to the church from the lych-gate at the top of the church path. From here the churchyard, fringed by old buildings and studded with stones recalling townsfolk long gone, stretches down to the red, sandstone church. On the left are the remains of the priory buildings, now private houses. Halfway down the path on the right are a stone stump and steps, all that remains of a medieval cross. Beyond is a spreading yew tree, revered as a symbol of ever-lasting life and believed to drive away storms raised by witches. The ornate west door replaced a plain arched doorway when the church was thoroughly restored in 1875 by W.H. Samson under the guidance of the architect G.E. Street. In the corner of the churchyard near the gateway into Church Street is the old Priest's House, rebuilt in 1875 and often inhabited in Victorian days by the Parish Clerk.

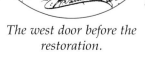

The west door before the restoration.

Enter the church through the porch, built about 1500. On entering the church for the first time the thing that impresses most is the near tangible atmosphere of calm. The church, though much altered, is the oldest building in the parish and has been central to the lives of Dunster people for at least 900 years. They have come to the church at the turning points of their lives, in the joy of marriage or christening and the grief of bereavement; in peace and war, bringing personal hopes and fears, nagging anxieties and fervent thanks – all the fragments that make up the patchwork of human existence.

There are many interesting and beautiful things to see in the church, yet it is not a museum but a living building sustained by daily worship. Visitors are always welcome to join this worship and to add their prayers to those offered here over the centuries. Everyone, whatever their belief or non-belief, will find an antidote to the speed and stress of modern living in the peace and quiet of this ancient building.

Once inside the main door it is hard to resist the temptation to walk to the centre of the nave and take a first look upward to the wide wagon roof (c.1500) and eastward towards the altar of the Parish Church and beyond.

After these first impressions, return to the main doors and turn to the left. At the back of the south aisle is the octagonal font (c.1530) with delicate carving that shows the instruments used in the crucifixion of Jesus and the wounds inflicted on his body. In the floor close by is a brass with two incised figures commemorating John and Agnes Wyther (1487). Above is a fine roof, once part of an earlier roof to the nave.

Move again to the centre of the nave. Turn your back on the screen and look to the west. The oldest part of the church, the Norman walls, can be seen in the north and west walls of the nave. The restored door we have already looked at from the outside. On the north wall is a Royal Coat of Arms of 1660, commemorating the restoration of the monarch, Charles II, who, while Prince of Wales, spent a night at Dunster Castle during the Civil War.

The medieval font.

Turn to face east and you will see the exceptional fan-vaulted rood-screen, the longest in England. It was built in about 1500 and placed here, two bays into the nave, to form a chancel for the parishioners, separate from that of the monks of the Benedictine priory. The rood-screen was so named because it usually supported a wooden rood (or crucifix) with figures of St Mary the Virgin and St John on either side. The projection in the centre at the back was to support an altar that was reached by a staircase set in the wall of the south aisle. The fan vaulting is deceptive; if you stand directly under the screen you will realise the screen's full width and strength.

Make your way to the eastern end of the church through the south door in the screen. Earlier screens once stood under the tower and the doorway at the head of the stairs leading to one of them can be seen in the north-west pillar of the tower. In the south transept is the gravestone of Adam of Cheddar, prior of Dunster c.1345–55, which was discovered in a fireplace in the Post Office. Between the transept and the aisle of the priory church, probably once the chantry chapel of St Lawrence, is an arch that dates back to c.1240 that was widened in the fifteenth or sixteenth century. The screen across it dates from c.1240 and was once part of the original screen under the eastern arch of the tower.

In this aisle are three interesting wooden chests. One has a slanting lid and is thought to have been originally a desk, used perhaps by the monks in the priory cloister. Another is a dugout chest of perhaps the twelfth century. The third, probably thirteenth century, is secured with iron bands. The last two each have five hasps and when they were used to house the parish valuables five padlocks kept everything safe. The vicar, the two churchwardens and the two overseers of the poor held the five keys, and all had to be present to unlock the chest – a simple ruse to deter dishonesty.

Against the south wall is an impressive monument with three recumbent figures: Thomas Luttrell and Margaret Hadley of Withycombe, his wife, and their daughter-in-law Joan Stewkley. George Luttrell, who put up the monument after the death of his mother, is shown kneeling. It is dated 1613. Set in the floor at the east end of the aisle is an alabaster slab with

St George's Church

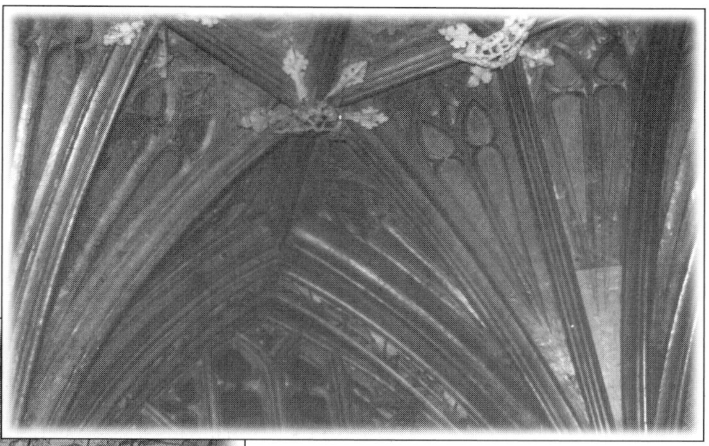

Right: *Detail of the fan vaulting in the rood-screen.*

Left: *The lower part of this arch was widened in the fifteenth or sixteenth century. The screen dates from c.1240 and was originally part of an earlier rood-screen.*

Right: *The parish chest, probably originating in the thirteenth century, was used to keep secure parish valuables such as the chalice and paten and the church registers and accounts.*

Inside St George's Church, looking east, c.1900.

an incised effigy and inscription to Lady Elizabeth Luttrell dated 1493. Both these monuments were moved here during the church restoration. On the north wall is a memorial tablet to Henry Maxwell-Lyte, keeper of the Public Records and historian of Dunster.

The choir of the priory church was thoroughly restored in 1875. Above the altar, with its medieval altar stone inscribed with five consecration crosses, are three thirteenth-century lancet windows which replace the Perpendicular east window which can be glimpsed in early photographs.

On the south wall is the effigy of a lady, probably Christian Segrave, wife of the fourth John de Mohun (c.1325). On the north side of the sanctuary are the mutilated effigies of Sir Hugh Luttrell (d.1428) and his wife Catherine Beaumont (d.1435). These lie on a much restored altar tomb with canopy (c.1500), which was probably designed originally for use as an Easter sepulchre.

Return to the nave of the Parish Church noting the brass plate of the alms box dated 1634 with the initials of the churchwardens, Matthew Haite and John Giles. In the north aisle the organ and trumpeting organ pipes dominate. Set in the floor is a brass plate economically commemorating first Edward Poyntes (1583) and later, in the eighteenth century, the three daughters of Giles Poyntz.

A doorway in the north-west pillar of the tower leads to the ringing chamber where visitors are welcome on Thursday evenings during practice hours. A door in the north transept (with a tendency to bang!) leads into the scented air of a garden set in the cloister of the old priory.

Above looms the great tower, which stands about 100 feet high. It was built in 1443 and from it at one, five and nine o'clock, day and night, a carillon plays out one of a number of tunes chosen in 1876 by Mr George Luttrell. A gate in the wall leads back to the road near the dovecote and tithe barn.

When Mr Gladstone visited the church in January 1877, he expressed his admiration for the restoration work and:

> *... was particularly struck with the combination which our church presents of grandeur with simplicity and ... that everything connected with it should be of the best ... Such testimony as this from one so qualified to give an opinion is very gratifying.*

Chapter Nine

STORIES & CUSTOMS

Dunster High Street, with Conygar Tower in the distance.

Dunster is a great place for stories. Some of these stem from misconceptions, written down by early travellers and chroniclers, then given the force of truth by repetition in later guidebooks. For instance, Bat's Castle, the Iron-Age fort, used to be called Caesar's Camp and is still often referred to as the Roman Camp not because of any very firm evidence of Roman occupation but because 'Roman' seems at one time to have been synonymous with 'very old'.

A – still current – story tells of the supposed secret tunnel running underground from Conygar Tower to Dunster Castle; perhaps linked in some way with the so-called priest hole in the King Charles bedroom and the secret stairs which were said to emerge by the stables. What an astonishing feat of engineering this would have been! When the Somerset Archaeological and Natural History Society visited the site in 1942 they apparently thought it to be less mythical than most tunnels. More than one informant has told me of the hollow sounds that seem to come from under Church Street when horses and carts passed over a certain spot; and interestingly, each witness described the 'rumble' or 'hollow sound' as coming from one and the same point under the street. The informants attributed the sounds to a tunnel, which they had known about since they were boys. They claimed that one of the great adventures of their school-days was to wriggle into the tunnel where it started on Conygar with lighted matches or tallow candles, the best thrill being the hundreds of bats that dangled from the roof about their heads.

Several members of the SANHS party scrambled down to explore the entrance to the cave but as it was blocked with debris no one was able to venture in to test the tale. Whether or not buses cause the same hollow rumble in Church Street today I don't know but I have always put down the possibility of a 'passage' under the street to either drains or a water supply dating from the time of the medieval priory.

Another tale that I have heard describes a cupboard that was apparently hidden behind the plasterwork in the wall of a cottage situated near the foot of the castle tor. When it was opened up, silver utensils were discovered inside which, so the story goes, 'belonged to the Luttrell family, and of course, were handed back at once.'

The opening up of communications between the West Street houses during the plague of 1645 is a long-established and dearly held tradition. The *Archaeological Journal* of 1858 includes this note from a correspondent in Bridgwater:

> *The occupants of the several tenements in a long street... established communications throughout its extent by opening doors internally from house to house, so as to avoid all necessity of going into the open street where the air was considered dangerous to life.*

This is delightfully referred to as an early 'Sanitary Regulation'. The position of several of these doorways can still be identified in the party-walls of a number of West Street houses. The openings would certainly have been utilised during the nineteenth century when flexible letting of houses seems to have been practised. A growing family needing more space was able to annexe rooms from an adjacent house occupied by only one or two elderly people, while larger houses sometimes accommodated more than one family.

There are few giants in Somerset folklore but Dunster can claim one, the benevolent Giant of Grabbist. He came up from Cornwall to Exmoor, so the story goes, to escape his unruly cousins. At first the townsfolk were afraid of him but once they realised that this was a gentle giant who meant no harm they became quite fond of him and, finding that their cattle and sheep were thriving, they even began to worry about what he was eating. It turned out that the Giant was fond of fish and he would wade into the Bristol Channel to scoop up huge shoals for his supper. Local fishing boats learnt to follow in his wake and made wonderful catches.

One day when the *Dorcas Jane*, captained by Elijah Crowcombe, had made such a catch and was filled with fish right up to the gunwales, a sudden storm blew up. The ship was tossed hither and thither and it was feared she would sink. However, the Giant stepped out, picked her up and popped her down safely in Watchet harbour 'all in a moment'.

Back in Dunster, the Giant's reputation grew. He'd return from sea, sit down on the hill dangling his feet in the River Avill on either side of the castle and wash the Severn mud off his legs. Then he'd climb to his chair on Grabbist. Folk would look out of their windows and wave to him 'and he'd wave back and there was all the week's washing – dried!'

Wassailing

Apple wassailing, the custom of visiting orchards to scare away evil spirits and ensure good crops, is still practised each year in the orchard of the Butcher's Arms in the neighbouring village of Carhampton on

Wassailing

Right: *Wassailing in Bond's Orchard, c.1950.*

Far right: *The gunfire is intended to scare off evil spirits.*

The Hobby Horse

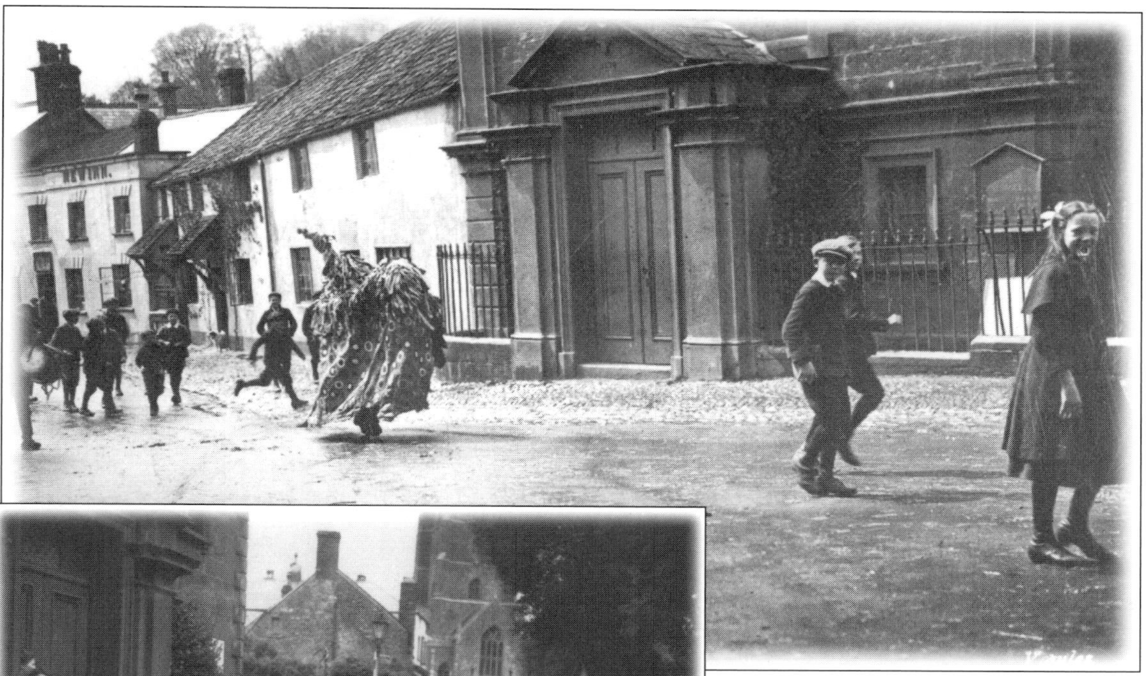

Above: *Alfred Vowles captures the essence of the May Day Hobby Horse Celebrations, c.1912.*

Above: *The Hobby Horse with musicians and gullivers outside the Methodist chapel in West Street, c.1950.*

Right: *Minehead Hobby Horse on its annual visit to Dunster, c.1978.*

17 January, Old Twelfth Night. After the singing of the wassail song, guns are fired into the trees, hot spiced cider is passed around, and toast, soaked in the mull, is placed in the branches 'for the robins'. In Dunster the custom continued in a similar way until the 1950s. The story goes that one year the wassailers, in an inebriated state, wassailed a pear tree by mistake and after this humiliation the custom was allowed to lapse.

The Hobby Horse

On May Day evening the Minehead Hobby Horse visits Dunster. In the earliest printed reference to the custom, Savage wrote in 1830 in the *Hundred of Carhampton*:

> *... they never fail to pay a visit to Dunster Castle, where, after having been hospitably regaled with strong beer and victuals, they always receive a present of money.*

The origins of the horse probably lie in the ancient May Day fertility celebrations though it has been suggested that the horse may commemorate a wreck or a phantom ship. Alternatively, it may have been used originally to scare away Viking raiders. It consists of a wide wooden frame that is carried on the shoulders of a man whose identity is concealed by sacking, brightly decorated with coloured circles

Carrying the Faggot

John Henry Burge carries in the ashen faggot at the Luttrell Arms Hotel, flanked by soldiers from the camp on Dunster Beach, c.1942.

and tassels of cloth. A central beribboned head with grotesque face and conical hat surmounts this. Gullivers, similarly dressed, and musicians accompany the horse which cavorts to the ceaseless drumbeat and compelling accordion melody known simply as 'The Hobby Horse Tune' or 'Sailor's Joy'. Like the pied piper the horse attracts adults and children alike, who follow, their fascination tinged with an element of apprehension.

The customary visit to Dunster is still practised although the Luttrells no longer live at the castle. The Minehead Sailors Horse has sired a number of progeny – the Town Horse, for example – and for a while Dunster had a horse of its own but it has not survived.

The Ashen Faggot

The custom of burning the ashen faggot used to be observed at Christmas in many West-Country homes. Legend says the custom originated after King Alfred's victory over the Danes at Ethandun when the conquering army feasted in the warmth of burning faggots of ash cut from the surrounding woodland. Another version suggests that the ash was cut and burnt after King Arthur's legendary victory at Cath-Brigion in Somerset.

The actual faggot is a large bundle of ash sticks, bound with whips of hazel or thorn and cut to fit the great open fireplaces. As the faggot burnt the bonds would snap and the party sitting around the fire would drink a toast and make wishes.

The practice is still carried out at the Luttrell Arms Hotel on Christmas Eve.

Carol Singing

Dunster has a long tradition of carol singing. There are several carols including the Dunster Carol which are still sung today by the group which continues to maintain the tradition.

Karl Meddick recalled his own experience of carol singing when he was a young man in the 1920s. He and his friend, Harry Lloyd, always spent Christmas Eve with 'Uncle' Dick Smith who lived in Park Street.

A good month or so before Christmas Uncle Dick would start to make preparations – he would make a small ashen faggot about a foot long and ensure that his rhubarb and parsnip wine – and cider – were in tip-top condition. In the evening Karl, with his father, mother and brothers, Ken and Harry, and Bob and Jack Witts, visited Uncle Dick's house. Here they sat around a big black stove and sang carols until 11.30p.m. when the Dunster carol singers arrived with Mr Jim Griffiths in charge. They'd all have a drink and then, when the church clock struck midnight, they would stand in Park Street and sing, 'Christians Awake! Salute the happy morn!'

Following this the group would all go up to the Luttrell Arms, kept at the time by Mr and Mrs Wrothe, where they would sing the old Dunster carols. Visitors staying at the hotel would come

Carol singing in Dunster, c.1976. Includes from foreground left: *Jack Furse, Geoff Dibble, Mike Dibble (in striped jacket), David Powles (with tin), Doug Dibble, Arthur Dyer (with checked cap) and John Case.*

down to join in and there was always a wonderful spread of sausage rolls, faggots and mince pies. Karl remembered particularly among the singers Mr Dibble, who lived at the Nunnery and had a habit of twirling the ends of his long moustaches, and Mr Lovell who lived at the Marsh and delivered the Sunday papers. It was usually 2a.m. before everyone began to make their way home.

Incidentally, Uncle Dick Smith used to scythe the grass in the old churchyard and Karl well remembers having to take him his tea wrapped up in a red handkerchief.

Rabbiting on Boxing Day was always popular.

A Mystery

Once upon a time a stone monument memorial to a horse stood in an orchard about 200 yards to the east of the Luttrell Arms Stables – now at the foot of the main car park. The story goes that during the Second World War the tomb was spotted, on land leased with the Luttrell Arms Hotel, by Captain Aylward Wyndham while taking part in a Home Guard exercise. The memorial consisted of an immense slab of slate three inches thick on which was built an altar tomb of Bath stone. The supporting panels were skilfully moulded and the longer sides adorned at each end with columns and capitals. The covering stone and several panels were missing but one with an inscription had been laid on the top. When the inscription had been cleaned it was found to read:

Nelson, My Favourite and Noble Horse, Born at Felbrigg, Norfolk in 1?40, Died at Dunster 3 May 1?56. S.W.

At first it was thought that the tomb might date from the sixteenth century and refer to some member of the Wyndham family who once owned Felbrigg. More careful investigation into the style of stonework and the lettering, however, suggested that it was likely to be much later – the dates were probably 1840 and 1856. During that period the Withycombe family kept the Luttrell Arms and for a while it was thought that S.W. might have been a member of that family but evidently nobody bore those initials and the general conclusion was that the horse had belonged to a visitor, almost certainly a lady.

Subsequently the name J. Pearse was discovered, faintly carved on the tomb, and this confirmed its dating to the mid-nineteenth century. Pearse was a local builder and craftsman in stone who worked on St Andrew's Church in Minehead and also created the Gothic and other architectural embellishment on what is now the Carlton Plume of Feathers.

A correspondent at the time of the discovery said that as a small boy, in about 1878, he had been intrigued by the monument and was told then that it had been set up by one of Dunster's doctors, a Dr Norman. It remains a mystery.

Chapter Ten

DUNSTER MARSH

The part of Dunster lying to the seaward side of the A39 is known as Dunster Marsh. In medieval times a road known as St Thomas' Street, and later as Rattle Row, led from the top of the High Street, past St Thomas' Chapel and rows of cottages down to Dunster Marsh; that part of the town devoted to the sea, shipbuilding and fishing.

We do not know just where the harbour was sited. If the sea once washed the foot of the castle tor, small boats may have been able to tie up there but it seems likely that once a wider mouth to the river Avill covered much of the area now known as the Hawn or haven. The course of the river has changed a good deal over the years and although the exact area of the harbour has not yet been identified we do know that the river and estuary gradually silted up and the port was eventually abandoned. The Avill has now been diverted and channelled in order to control the flooding that used to occur regularly, sometimes leaving houses at the Marsh under water for days on end.

During the medieval period marshland lay on either side of the river, some of which was used for wild fowling, some as common grazing land. In the middle of this area, near the river on a firm piece of ground, was a house of some importance now known as Lower Marsh. As early as 1266 Agnes of Marsh held a furlong of land for which she paid a rent of 16 capons at Christmas and Easter. In the 1400s the wealthy Ryvers family lived at Marsh.

Swans at the Hawn.

Floods

Left: *Margaret Tudball took this picture of the flooded marshes in 1949 when she worked for the Minehead photographer Kingsley Taylor.*

Below: *Until the 1960s flooding was a regular occurrence in Dunster until a new channel was built for the River Avill. Houses at Marsh were frequently flooded as were these cottages near Gallox Bridge.*

Above: *Cars grind to a halt on the flooded main road near Loxhole Bridge.*

Some places change little over the years. Left: *The Old Manor House at Dunster Marsh, then known as Lower Marsh, in the nineteenth century.* Right: *The Old Manor House, c.1930.*

John, as woodward to the Luttrells, held a house and 20 acres of land. He paid among other dues, the 16 capons. His brother Robert was bailiff and steward and was in a position to lend large sums of money to Dame Margaret Luttrell.

The house passed then to John Loty whose family held the property for three centuries. The first John Loty was constable at the castle and the family retained these links of service. At the end of the century John Loty III was the largest holder of burgages in Dunster and it could be that his wealth made him unpopular. One violent day in 1487 after Hugh Luttrell's pound at Nether Marsh was broken into and 20 ewes stolen, a group of men prepared an ambush for John Loty with the intention of murdering him. It was unsuccessful.

The earliest parts of the present house at Lower Marsh and the chapel over the porch were probably built at this time.

John's successor, Robert Loty, left a widow, Joan, who married as her third husband John Luttrell who lived for a while at the Priory after its closure. Unusually they were granted a divorce and Joan married yet again but John Luttrell does not seem to have been willing to let her go easily. He is said to have persecuted her, stealing sheep, killing doves, raiding the house for goods and flooding the lower part of the house by breaking down nearby dykes. The family was boycotted and, though some of the acts may be fictitious, John Luttrell's description of Joan as the supposed 'wyeff' of Peter Fauntleroy maybe throws a little light on the episode. The chapel was in use at this time, for Joan had a domestic chaplain though John prevented him from saying Mass by carrying off the chalice.

In 1510 the whole estate passed to the Poyntz family of Devon, who continued as devout Roman Catholics and who owned property at Leigh Barton and Leighland and contributed to the maintenance of a priest there. They continued to use the chapel over the porch at Marsh after the Reformation. By 1760, the Poyntz lands in Dunster and Carhampton had been let for some years, so the family decided to sell both them and the house to Henry Fownes Luttrell for £2,400. They remained the property of the Luttrell estates until the estate was sold in 1954.

In 1874 the West Somerset Railway was extended to Minehead from Watchet. The line, broad gauge, crossed the Marsh and a station was soon built by William Harrison for £912. Much of the ballast for the

Dunster Station staff 1943–44.
Mr Kemp (signalman),
Roy Hobbs (clerk),
F.J. Hunt (signalman),
Mrs E.L. Hunt (crossing-keeper),
Sid Cole (stationmaster),
Lena Moss (porter),
Mr Hobbs (porter/shunter).

Dunster Station

Right: *F.J. Hunt (Jim) (signalman) and Don Spencer (porter), 1959.*

Left: *Upgrading Sea Lane Crossing, 1959. Signal gantries are being altered for gates to be placed across the line instead of across the road.*

Right: *Signalman Jim Hunt has just received the 'key' from the driver before the train can proceed to Minehead.*

Left: *Jim Hunt outside the signal box, 1959. The signals are now controlled from Minehead.*

line was provided from the castle estate, sand was taken from the beach and gravel from the field beside the Sea Lane crossing known as the 'Ballasto' field. The line was converted to narrow gauge over the last weekend of October 1882 and in 1897 the Minehead Railway was amalgamated with the Great Western Railway. Regular trains brought customers to market and took shop and office workers and schoolchildren to Minehead and Taunton. Holiday-makers – as well as polo players with their horses – travelled by rail from all over the country directly to Dunster and during the Second World War, when the military used the trains, the station employed seven staff: stationmaster, clerk, porter, two signalmen, and a porter/shunter, as well as the crossing-keeper who operated the gates at the Sea Lane level crossing by hand.

In Dunster signal box, 1966. Jim Hunt (left) *and Norman Snell.*

In 1971 the line was closed but was opened again as a private concern in 1976 by the West Somerset Railway Association who today successfully run steam-hauled trains in addition to diesel services during the summer months.

Many of the holiday-makers who travelled by train stayed in chalets on Dunster Beach. The first of these 'mini homes from home' or 'bungalettes' were built by the Dunster Trading and Transport Company during the 1920s and '30s. These wooden buildings were prefabricated in a sawmill and workshop housed near the old barn, now Avill Court, at Dunster Marsh. Under the supervision of foreman, Walter Frost, workers Reg Vaulter, Bert Packman and Bert Hole, together with Ken Meddick who joined them a little later, constructed the simple buildings ready to be taken to the beach for erection. When the first one had been put up it had to be taken down again and re-erected because it was in view of the castle. By 1935 the huts, which cost about £80 each, had proved so popular with visitors that 94 had been completed and sold.

During the Second World War the huts were commandeered, first as temporary accommodation for evacuees and later by the Army – including Royal Engineers, Pioneer Corps, Somerset Light Infantry and Royal Artillery – who were all involved in building and maintaining sea defences and in training. Then in 1942 the Americans arrived and encamped at Dunster Beach while practising tank manoeuvres and gunnery on North Hill in readiness for D-Day. At the start roads, cook-houses, messes, more showers and lavatories were built on the Dunster Beach site while the huts were used for sleeping and living accommodation; an Army stove was installed in the centre of each. Four men were assigned to a hut but eight cohabited in times of pressure when they would sleep clockwise as in a bell tent, toes close to the source of

The Beatles' train – 'A Hard Day's Night' – passing through Dunster Station in 1964.

warmth. Early on in the war some of the Dunster Beach chalets were commandeered as an Army Rest Centre with a new intake of troops every fortnight. The vicar of Dunster, the Revd A.H. Balleine, was very keen that a canteen should be provided for the soldiers and so the WI was asked to undertake the organisation and provision of meals and to run the canteen. Meals were provided each night in the Memorial Hall from 6.30p.m. to 9.30p.m. on weekdays and 4p.m. to 9.30p.m. on Sundays. Every night there was plenty of food – eggs and beans, apple pies, blancmanges, tarts and cakes. Up to 19 November 1940 it is reported that 8,596 meals were cooked and 11,598 cups of tea served. The canteen was extremely popular and soldiers came, night after night, to enjoy home cooking and female company. The canteen continued to do good work until 1942.

Left: *American soldiers at the castle in 1944. They are pictured with Mr Southam, the butler, 1936–45.*

Right: *The Home Guard on Castle Hill, 1943.* Left to right, back row: *Ossie Gould, Gerald Sully, Stan Ladd, Bert Davey, Jim Copp, Chris Champion;* centre: *Reg Vaulter, Roy Sully, Jack Jones, Charlie Welsh, George Needs, Fred Hunt;* front: *Harold Gill, Don Vaulter, Cliff Rowe, Tom Winter, Ken Radford, Mr White.*

Left: *One of the Home Guard platoons.*

Towards the end of the war the people of Dunster collected over £1,000 (£20,000 by today's reckoning) to help the people of Elst in the Netherlands, which had been liberated by troops of the Wessex Division among whom were two Dunster men, William Dainton and Wesley Gould. This picture shows representatives from Elst with Wes (front row, second from right) *and Bill* (front row, right) *on a visit in 1992.*

It was not until 1946 that Dunster Beach was handed back to Geoffrey Luttrell by the War Office and the chalets returned to their anxious owners. Inevitably many were in 'a disgraceful state' but owners soon put things to rights and were able to enjoy their unique brand of seaside holiday again. With the break-up of the Dunster Castle Estates in 1951 the Beach was sold to Mr Herbert Kempson Reeves, a businessman who had retired to Hacketty Way in Porlock before the Second World War. He ran the business under the unappealing name of Hutlands Ltd (later to be improved to Beachlands!). This was a time of insecurity for chalet owners who feared the commercial exploitation of the site but eventually Mr Reeves decided to sell up. The Chalet Owners Association met, agreed that they must do their best to acquire the enterprise and after a difficult struggle were finally able to raise the money needed. The sale was completed in December 1965 and Dunster Beach Holidays Ltd became the new owners. Dunster Beach continues to be owned collectively with the interests of the chalet owners at heart. A recent two-part television programme shared the idyllic pleasures of owning a chalet on Dunster Beach with the general public.

Enjoying the sand and sea at Dunster Beach, 1950s.

Dunster Beach

Right: *Relaxing beside their 'bungalette'.*

Left: *Dunster Beach chalets in the 1950s. In the background can be seen a pillbox put up during the war.*

Right: *Timothy Bourne Whitby lived in his shack beside the main entrance to Dunster Beach for nearly 20 years. He was a man of education who had trained as a jockey and who, on the death of his wife, became a vagrant. He came to Dunster in the late 1930s and was held in affection by people from all walks of life who had occasion to pass his home. He was befriended by holiday-makers at the beach and by Mr and Mrs Hunt and their daughter Margaret at nearby Crossing Bungalow. He enjoyed visits to the castle where he discussed all matters equine with Mr Geoffrey Luttrell while Mrs Luttrell kept a caring eye on him. He had a talent for painting, particularly horses, and an especial knack for painting on glass. During the war the authorities tolerated Tim – in spite of a brush with the law over the matter of disappearing Army coal! He was popular with the soldiery. In the 1950s the new owner of Dunster Beach had plans for expansion and offered Tim £50 to move away. Fortunately the plans did not materialise and Tim soon moved back and reconstructed his home. As he aged and became frail Mr and Mrs Luttrell offered him the opportunity to put his shack closer to the castle where he lived until his death. He is buried in Dunster and is remembered as a remarkable man.*

Chapter Eleven

SHOPPING IN DUNSTER

Above: *West Street, c.1935.* From right: *Stagshead House, G.O. Bond (butcher), the New Inn, Grant's shop, Hawker's bakery.*

Until the Second World War – and even a little later – you could buy everything you wanted in Dunster. John Haydon, born in February 1908, remembered many of the old businesses in the town; as a youngster he worked for a while at Parham's Dunster Supply Stores driving the pony and trap to outlying cottages and farms.

John remembered from the 1920s Miss Lock's shop and Mr Brook's paper shop in the High Street, as well as Harry Eames' butchers shop (Harry Eames lived at the Marsh near his slaughterhouse). In West Street was Bond's (butchers), Councer's grocery shop (later Grant's) and Mrs Hawker's bakery. Here Clem Sparkes was head baker assisted by Shaver Court, Bert Caddy, Jesse Woodbury, Ray Jones and Ernie Hurford who also delivered bread around the area. Bill Long kept a little china shop while Jimmy Tame's wife kept another grocery shop.

Parham's

Hilda Parham recalls Parham's, the village grocery in 1935, the year she married Jack Parham and moved to Dunster:

In the 1930s there were four grocers in Dunster; two large, by village standards, and two small. The small ones – Mrs Miller's in Water Street (Park Street) and Mrs Tame's in West Street opposite Lamacraft's Riding Stables – were managed by the women while their husbands went out to work. Mrs Tame also sold china and, during the war years, sold the pies provided through the Food Ministry to supplement the rations in the countryside where there were no canteens or British restaurants. Another larger shop, also in West Street, was kept by the two Grant brothers and their wives.

Dunster Shopping

The building in the centre was the parish workhouse until c.1840.

Below: *Lily Tame, Mrs Tame and Granfer Tame outside their shop in West Street, c.1928.*

Right: *Before 1901 Dunster Supply Stores were owned by the Amor family.*

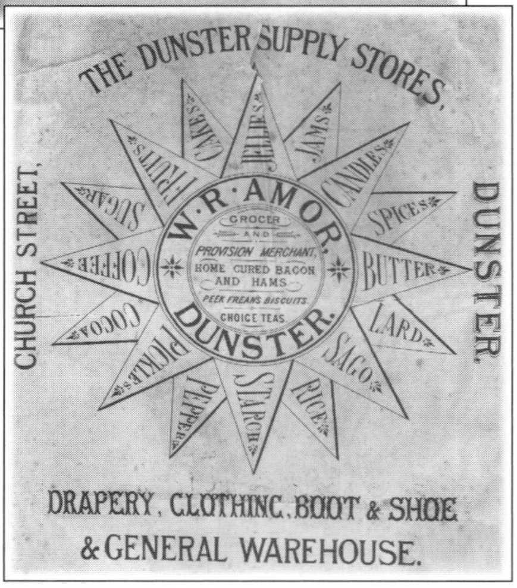

Below: *Mrs Haydon (Violet Goacher's mother) on the right talking to the future Mrs Jim Griffiths (senr) who worked in the shop, c.1912.*

Dunster Stores

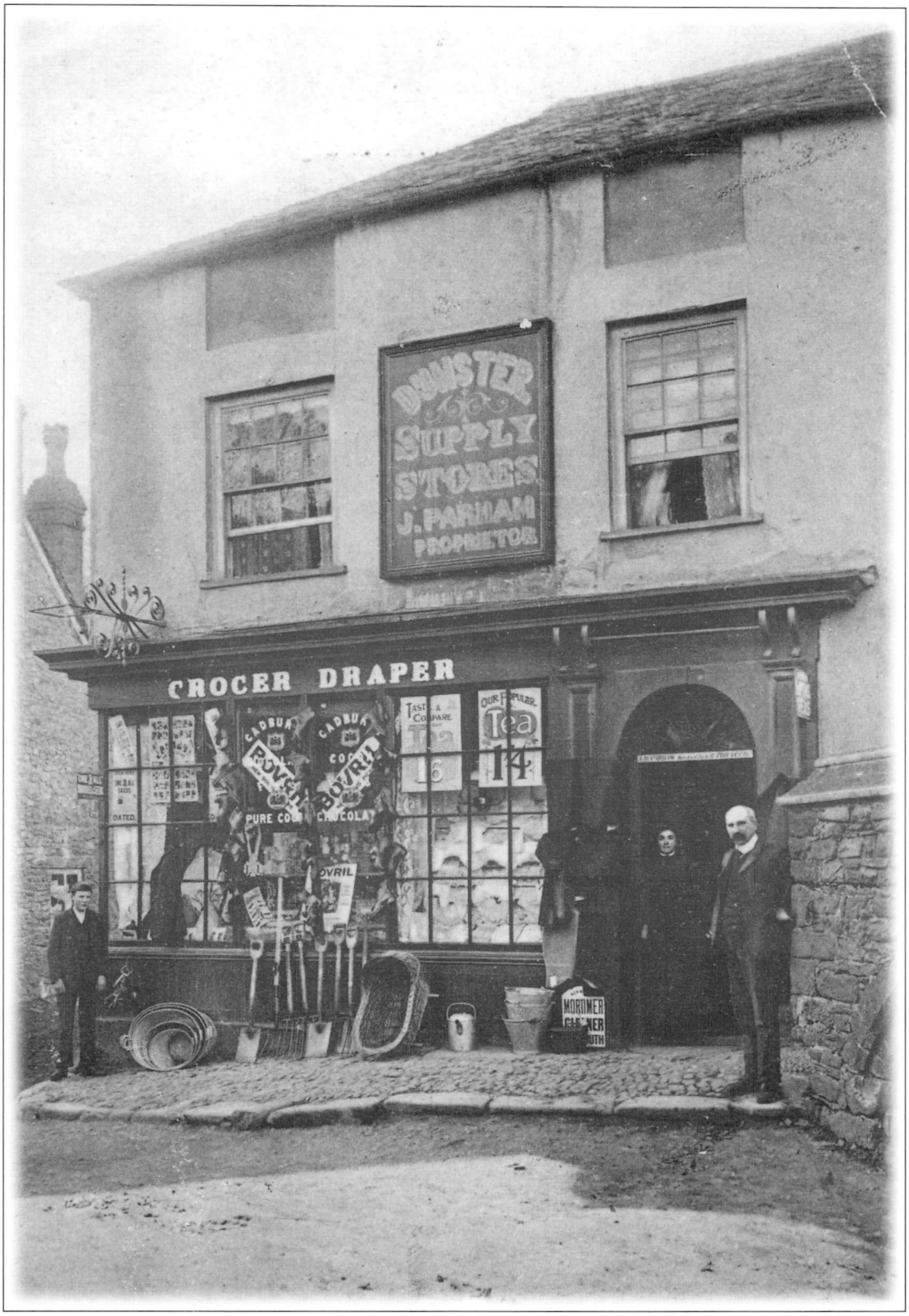

Dunster Supply Stores (Parham's) some time between 1901, when J.H. Parham bought the business, and 1911. John Henry Parham is on the pavement and in the doorway is Kate Cavill whom he later married. The boy may be 'Budget' Winter who drove the wagon.

A Miscellany of Goods & Services

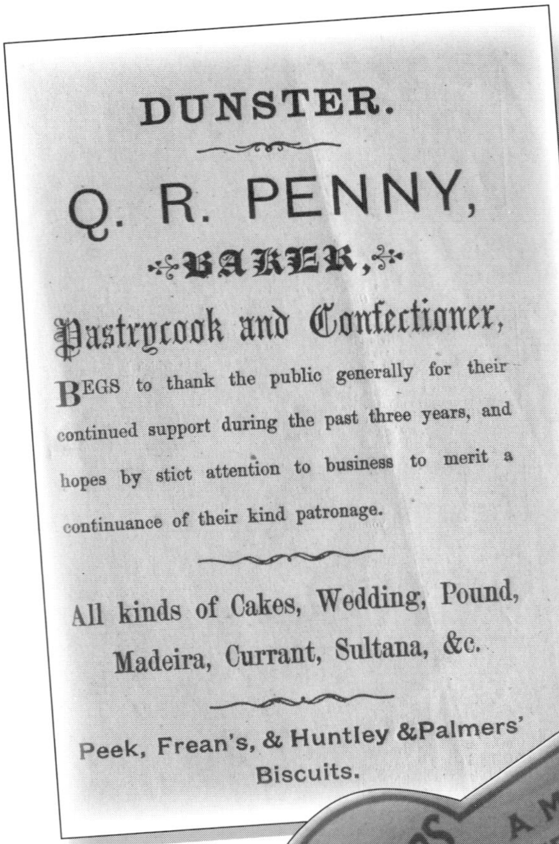

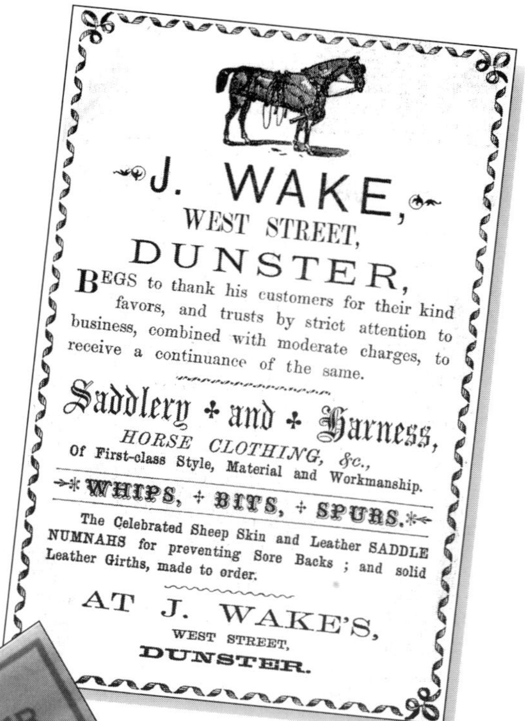

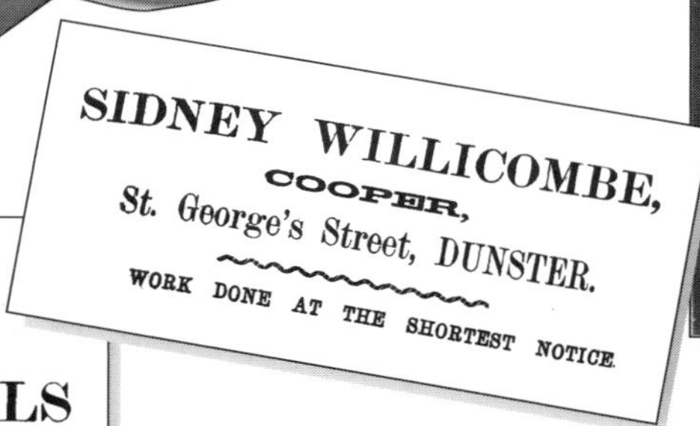

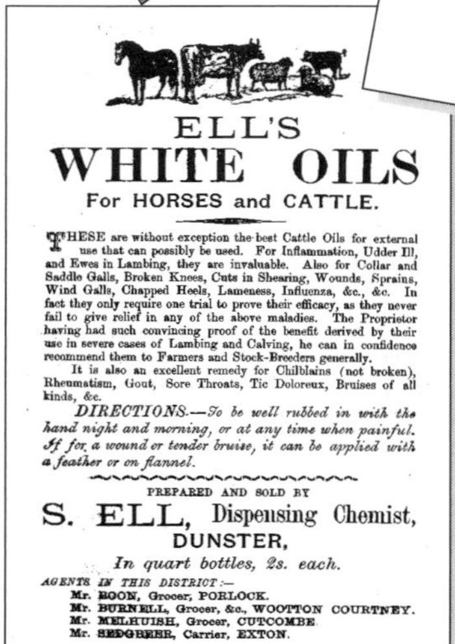

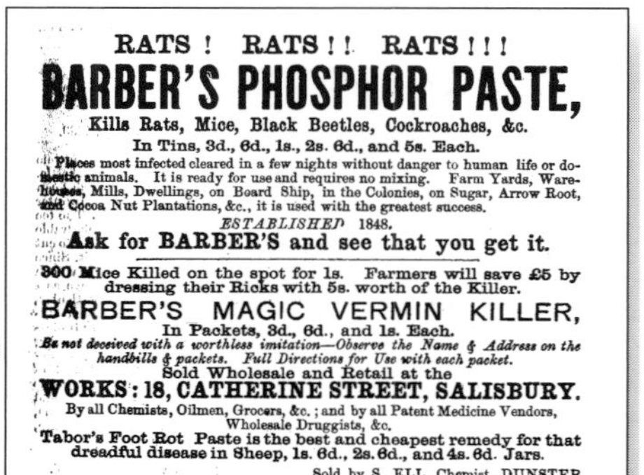

Our shop – a larger one – was in Church Street at the corner next to the arch in the churchyard wall which itself had once, round about 1682, been let out as premises for a shop or stall at a rent of 1s. a year. Our shop frontage was Victorian although its history as a shop was almost certainly older than that.

When I first knew it the shop seemed quite dark and on entering one was assailed by a mixture of smells – fruit, vegetables, spices, coffee, leather and even paraffin. In front of you was a long mahogany counter running the length of the shop with a shorter piece at one end at right angles. Various tempting piles of goods were stacked along it with a basket of figs or fruit in season. At intervals were spaces where assistants could take customers' orders or serve them as they waited, seated on wooden chairs. A Shops Act demanded that these seats were provided so that assistants could take a rest – but they never seemed to be used in that way!

Just inside the door were rolls of floor covering – various qualities and patterns of lino and coconut matting. At the end of the shop was the drapery section. Here everything for everyday wear could be bought – underwear for men, women and children; corsets, liberty bodices, etc. Some years earlier material for men's shirts had also been stocked ready for their womenfolk to make into shirts. There were cottons, needles, scissors, tape, elastic and knitting wool. One lady told me that the sock wool – Tulip brand – was so good that she was still wearing stockings she had knitted 20 years earlier – for when the 'veet' did wear out she said, 'I do re-voot 'em and when the legs did wear out I do re-leg em.'

The ironmongery section sold everything for the house – anything not in stock was soon procured for customers had to be satisfied. Farming essentials were also stocked – rakes, milking buckets, saws, hob-nailed boots and leggings.

Another section provided women's shoes and slippers and children's boots and shoes. About 80 years earlier there had been 13 boot- and shoemakers in the village and in 1935 there was still one. Tom Elliott still bought his leather, tingles, small nails and heelballs from us for repairs, as did several other men who walked in from Luxborough and Timberscombe.

Hilda Parham.

The floor was wooden and covered with a fine sprinkling of sawdust. This smothered any fat or anything wasted in the continual weighing and wrapping of loose goods. The floor was swept each day and new sawdust sprinkled. Double crates of oranges, when in season, stood on the floor as did bags of onions and Rodhuish swedes, which were considered superior to those grown in less red soil. Long wooden rods were suspended along the ceiling from which various goods were hung – from aprons and men's cord or tweed trousers to brushes, pails and even a hip bath.

Below the counter at the back were deep drawers holding loose currants (5d., 6d. and 7d. a pound), sultanas (ditto), raisins, mixed peel, demerara sugar, soft brown and pieces. The wooden fixtures ran from floor to ceiling, the upper ones arched to hold the tall tins for teas and coffee beans, while the lower part had smaller drawers than those under the counter designed to hold two qualities of rice – pudding rice and patna for curries. There was also bullet sago and tapioca, macaroni, dried peas and yellow splits and lentils. All these goods had to be weighed and packed by hand, many with their own special colour paper bag. Biscuits were also sold loose

The horse-drawn delivery van, driven by 'Budget' Winter, with Eddo Thomas holding the oil measure.

Eddo with Parham's first motorised delivery van. Eddo never worked anywhere else.

and were displayed in glass-topped tins along special wooden racks.

When I first knew the shop in 1935 the delivery man was Edwin Thomas (Eddo) – he drove the horses and later the motorised delivery vans. He first came to work in the shop on Saturdays and after school when he was ten years old. He swept the pavement, cleaned the large brass scales and rode the carrier bicycle around the village. At one time the Carhampton deliveries were done by handcart. Eddo served in the First World War and was gassed, though not badly, and afterwards returned to his old job, which he did until he retired.

At that time there was no electricity or gas in the country villages. Cooking was done on the kitchen range or on oil-fired cookers and of course there were oil lamps and candles for light. This meant that we sold many gallons of paraffin. We supplied customers in Carhampton, Withycombe, Rodhuish, Roadwater, Luxborough, Cutcombe, Bridgetown, Exton and Winsford. So much paraffin was sold in Winsford that our supplier left drums of oil for us to distribute in the village, as we could not carry enough in the van even though we went there twice a week.

We went to the villages on one day to take orders, sell dresses, shoes, shirts, etc., from samples and buy rabbits, butter, cream, potatoes and turnips – indeed anything that could be sold again. I remember Mr Thomas bringing home a broody hen, a piglet and a puppy that he had a commission for.

There was a lot of difference in the quality of the butter – some of it had not been beaten long enough so it was too watery and some would not keep because it lacked salt. My mother-in-law saved the best butter for her favourite customers. As well as farmhouse butter we sold a lot of butter from New Zealand. This came in in 28lb boxes, which were very strong and well made – they served as excellent storage units when stacked one on top of the other.

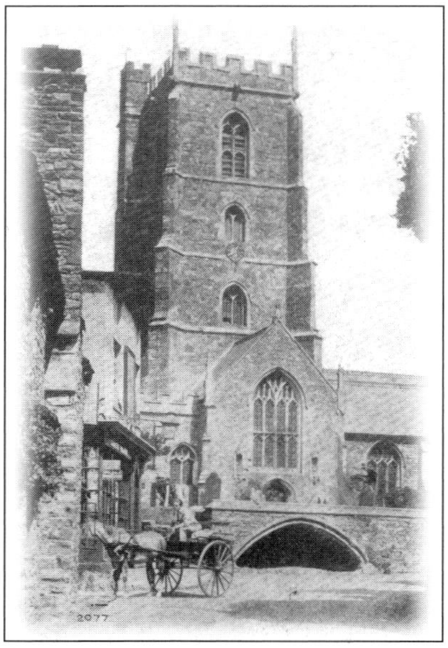

Shopping at Parham's in the 1930s.

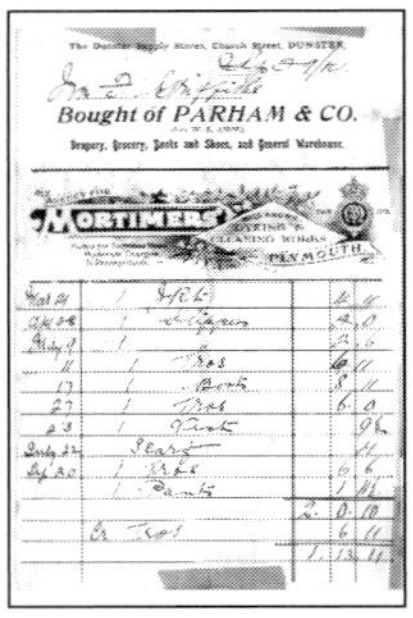
Bought of PARHAM & CO.

We spent long hours patting the butter into pounds and half pounds. In our second warehouse we had a large table which had originally been the kitchen table in the Luttrell Arms Hotel. This was covered with a huge marble slab. We had two sets of butter pats, a bucket of water, a pair of scales, a long wire to cut the butter block and sheets of real greaseproof paper cut to size. We had four people working. One cut the butter from the block, one weighed it to exact weight, one patted – dipping the pats into the water (which was constantly changed) – and one wrapped it and packed it back into the boxes. Good working on the butter meant that the flavour improved.

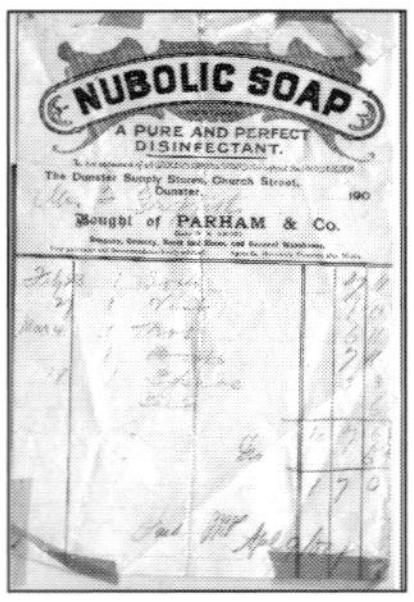
NUBOLIC SOAP
A PURE AND PERFECT DISINFECTANT.
Bought of PARHAM & Co.

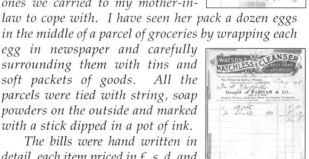

Lard also came in large blocks and was cut with a long cheese wire with handles at each end. The lard was pressed into shape. We also weighed various brown sugars, rice, etc., dried fruit, biscuits and flour. There was no sellotape nor plastic bags nor sticky labels, so everything had its own special wrap, identified by type and colour of paper or bag, as well as the method of wrapping. There were few cardboard boxes and most parcels were wrapped in paper. This was quite an art. Any tricky ones we carried to my mother-in-law to cope with. I have seen her pack a dozen eggs in the middle of a parcel of groceries by wrapping each egg in newspaper and carefully surrounding them with tins and soft packets of goods. All the parcels were tied with string, soap powders on the outside and marked with a stick dipped in a pot of ink.

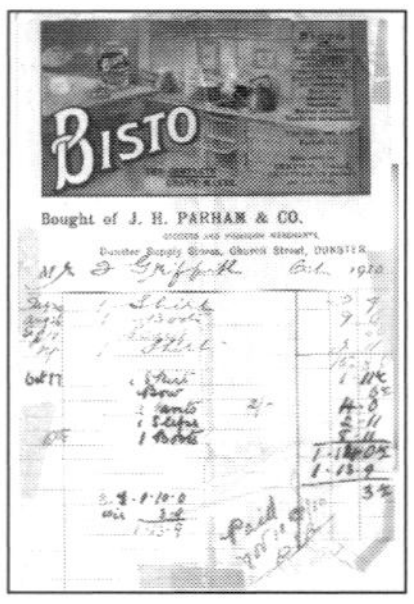
BISTO
Bought of J. H. PARHAM & CO.

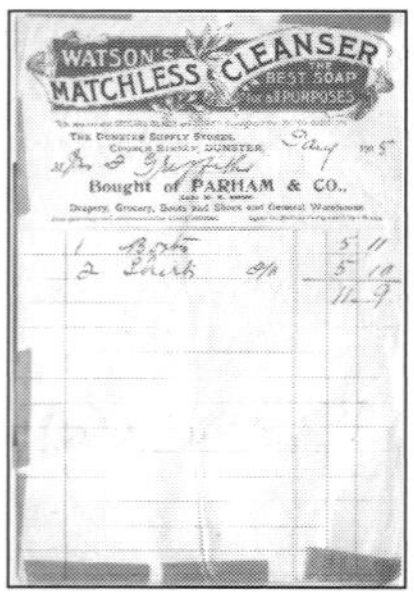
WATSON'S MATCHLESS CLEANSER
BEST SOAP
Bought of PARHAM & CO.

The bills were hand written in detail, each item priced in £. s. d. and added – young people who came to work at 14 years of age needed months of practice before their calculations could really be relied on.

As well as Mr Thomas, we had working in 1935 Arthur Yeandle, Howard Burnett, Stan Duddridge, Miss Elsie Woodbury, Miss Edna Ladd and an errand boy. We opened the shop at 8a.m. – the assistants coming in at this time had breakfast and tea. We closed daily at 7p.m., 9p.m. on Saturdays, with a half day on Wednesdays. I think there was only one week's

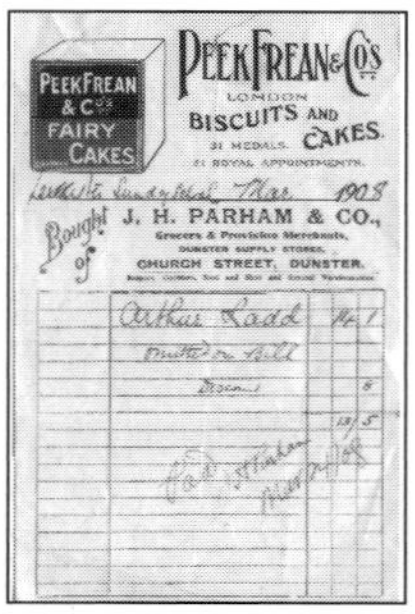
PEEK FREAN & Co's
LONDON
BISCUITS AND CAKES
PEEK FREAN & Co FAIRY CAKES
Bought of J. H. PARHAM & CO.,
CHURCH STREET, DUNSTER.

Parham's bills.

holiday a year. The shop was always closed on Sundays, Bank Holidays and Good Friday. It was unheard of for any unnecessary work to be done on Holy Days or Sundays; a woman was looked down upon if there was washing on the line on those days unless she had a new baby. My father never went to work on Old Christmas Day, 6 January, and he always prepared the Sunday vegetables on Saturdays, and cleaned the boots and shoes.

Nearly all the cottagers kept poultry in their back gardens and sometimes also a pig.

In one of our warehouses we kept large wooden vats containing wheat, maize and layers mash. These were sold in large brown paper bags holding either 7 or 3½lbs. We also sold Karswood Poultry Spice in small packets. This was added to the wet mash and vegetable mixture in order to encourage laying. Chickens were hatched under broody hens and a china egg was kept in the nest boxes to encourage hens to use them. Empty orange crates were in great demand for this purpose.

Jack Parham, delivering groceries in the High Street, raises his hat to photographer, Miss Prior, at the Bantam Shop over the road.

About once a year we ordered a load of 28lb bars of salt for salting in the cottagers' pigs. The pigs were killed on site and dressed and cured by an unofficial pig killer who travelled around the district. A barrel of cider was considered a necessary help on these occasions. The salt came on the train and was stacked in the salt house – a dry area in what had once been a passage. A special galvanised saw was kept for the purpose of cutting the bars to the size required. All the old people preferred the bar salt – when ground-up salt came on sale they declared that it would not salt their pig meat successfully. Most of the pig killing was done at the same time of year, the hotter times being avoided, and we made special deliveries with only salt all around the area.

John Haydon recalled that at one time many people kept pigs and that there were salterns on the left side of the castle gatehouse where sides of bacon and ham were salted and sweet pickled.

Parham's shop continued through until the 1970s, son Jack taking over from his father in 1934. During the war years Jack Parham was in the Observer Corps and in spare moments at the lookout on the beach at the end of the golf course he would count out the tiny coupons collected from customers each week. The night that someone opened the door and they all blew away is best not remembered!

From the 1970s things changed. People no longer expected to buy all the basics in their villages but were beguiled by the goods on offer in the new supermarkets. Motor transport for everyone meant that people no longer relied on deliveries. Among the shops in Dunster that closed for good at this time were Bond's butchers in West Street and, inevitably, Parham's of dear memory.

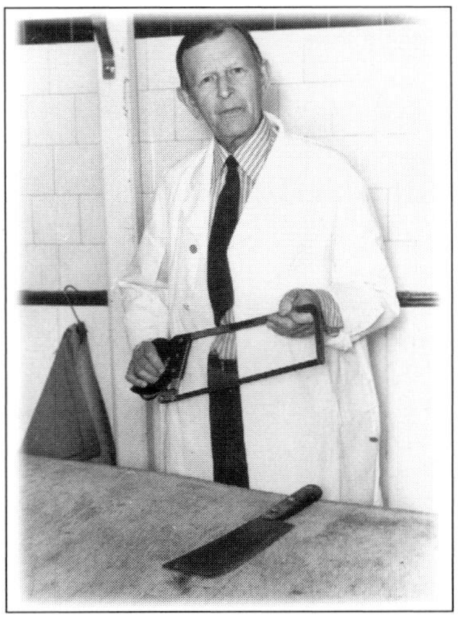

Bond's, butchers, in West Street. In 1977 Gordon Bond gave up the business after three generations.

Edgar Dyer, Saddler

Muriel Petford writes of her father and of growing up in Dunster in the 1920s:

Edgar Dyer was born in 1894 and was three months old when his parents, Thomas and Mary, moved to Dunster with older brother Arthur and sister Bertha, who died during the First World War aged 21. Edgar went to the Methodist School in West Street where they paid a penny a week. When it closed he attended the Church School, where he completed his education. (Incidentally, work on Dunster School recently revealed an exercise book of my father's under the floorboards and dated 1907.) With the amalgamation of the scholars, my grandfather was elected to the School Board to represent the Nonconformists and when he retired my father replaced him and served for over 30 years.

On leaving school my father was apprenticed to the saddlery trade and served his apprenticeship at Ernest Norman's main shop in North Street, Taunton, as my grandfather was then managing the Dunster branch.

When my father completed his apprenticeship, work was hard to find so in 1912 he and a number of lads from Dunster and the surrounding district emigrated to Canada to seek work. Dad did various jobs in Canada and the USA, but when war was declared in 1914 he returned to England and joined the 12th Hussars and did most of his service in Mesopotamia. Although he had intended to return to Canada after the war, he was persuaded to join his father in the saddler's shop and married in 1920. Grandfather became owner of the

Right: *Edgar and Lilly Dyer with neighbour Phyllis Morris enjoying a Sunday afternoon out in the pony and trap during the Second World War.*

Above: *Advertisement card for E. Dyer.*

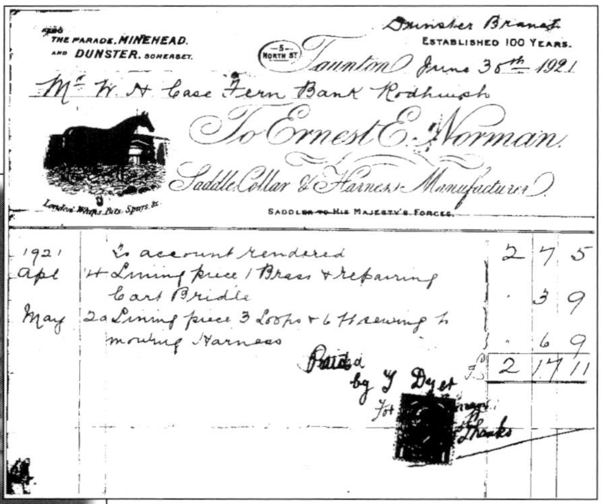

Above: *Billhead from Ernest Norman.*

Left: *Thomas Dyer* (left) *with Edgar Dyer outside the shop some time in the late 1920s. The saddlery dated back to 1712.*

Mr and Mrs Harry Stradling. Harry was Dunster's much-loved last blacksmith.

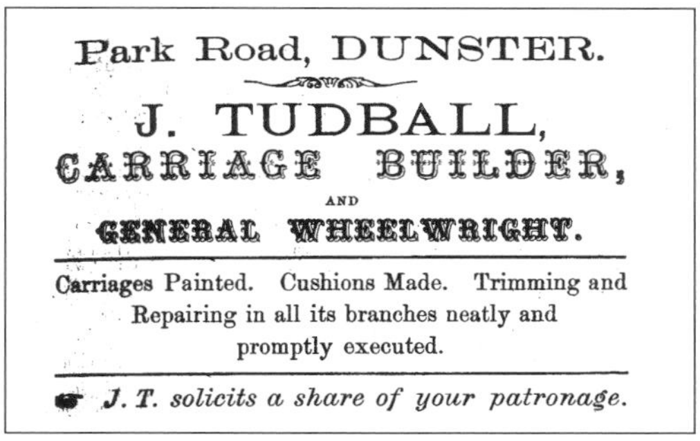

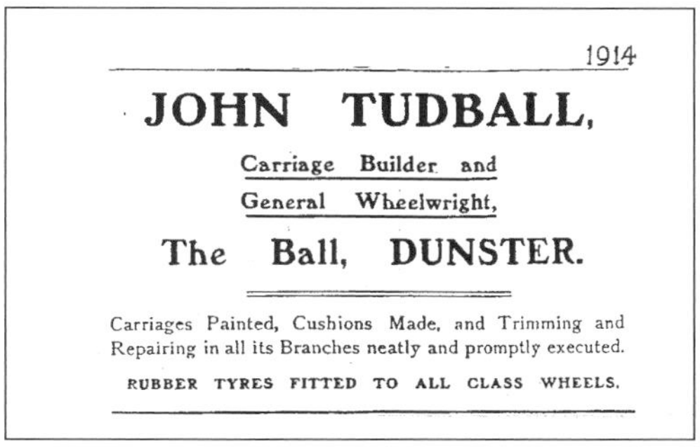

Advertisements for Tudball wheelwrights, Dunster.

business in about 1922 and 'ran' it until he retired in 1930 when my father took it over until his death in 1975.

During the Second World War father was a member of the Observer Corps – a 'lookout' was set up on Dunster Beach. He never drove a car but loved to ride his horse over the hills. Our house in the High Street had stabling at the rear.

I was born in 1921 and my brother Eric in 1923. We both went to Dunster School at the age of three. We walked to school around the Priory Green, and on our way home would often call at the old tithe barn where the carpenters carried out work for the Dunster Castle estate. Walter Long would find us a piece of wood and a small plane to keep us amused. Further along the road we would look in on the smithy – Harry Stradling would be shoeing the heavy cart-horses and at the end of the Ball were Bill Tudball and Frank Quick, wheelwrights, who would be making wheels for farm carts.

The Luttrell Arms Hotel was run by the Evereds in those days and every Good Friday morning they brought out trays of hot-cross buns – one for every child in the village. I left Dunster School in 1932, having passed the 11+ examination for Minehead County School.

My mother, Lillian, was born in Bristol in 1884 – her father, James Ell, having gone from Dunster to work as a cabinet-maker in the city. She spent her school holidays at Dunster with her grandparents at the chemist's shop in Church Street. On leaving school she was apprenticed to a Bristol milliner and after her marriage in 1920 was able to use her sewing ability, stitching linen linings to saddles. She was 80 when my father died and continued to run the shop unaided until she was 89. To give her a 'send off' in 1984, the Masters of the West Somerset Hunt and the Minehead Harriers arranged a joint meet outside the Luttrell Arms, in her honour. She died at Malvern in 1989 at the age of 94 and is buried at Dunster with my father.

The Dyers

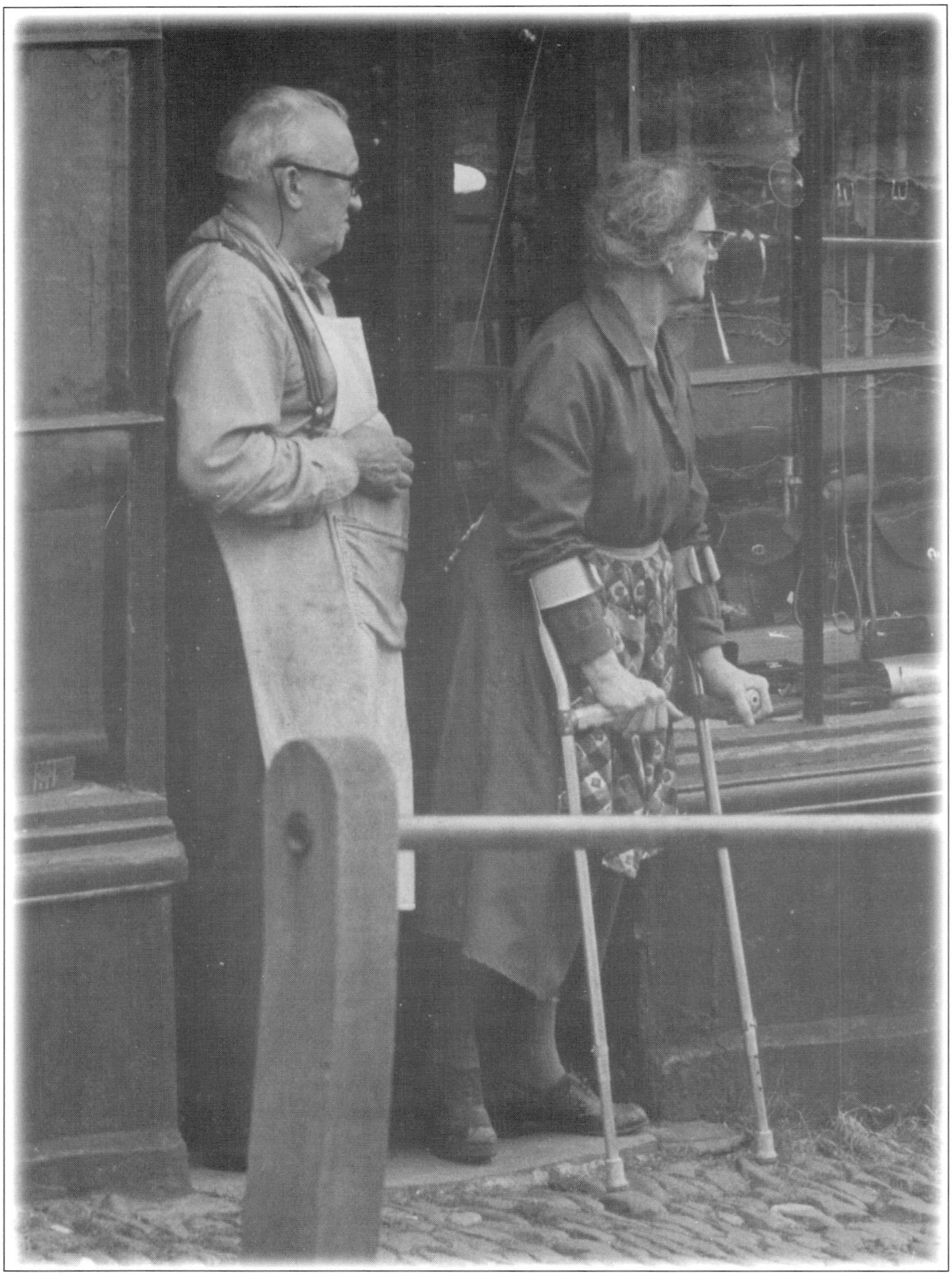

Edgar and Lillian Dyer outside the saddlery, c.1974.

Chapter Twelve

GROWING UP IN THE 1930S & '40S

The Magic Book of Nursery Rhymes. Agnes Burgess Concert, c.1937.
Left to right, back row: *Joan Symonds, Eric Tarr, Doris Tudball, Margaret and Kathleen Burge;*
front: *Connie Griffiths, Hedley Dyer, Peter Tudball, Aubrey and Norman Case, Ruth Payne.*

Peter Tudball was born in August 1929, at Conygar View. He recalls:

Our house at Conygar View, built in 1927, was very basic. We had a black cooking range in the kitchen-cum-living room; gas and electricity were brought to the house later. It must have been a real joy to my parents having these services available – electric lighting with a single two-pin point for an electric iron (250 watts and not earthed!), and a gas cooker, with shilling slot meters. I just remember the oil lamps and the warmth they provided. We did have a bathroom with running cold water. The hot water came from a copper boiler in the kitchen, heated by coal, and was carried to the narrow bath, which did not need much to fill it. A gas boiler and a wall-mounted electric water heater came later. Bath night was only on a Saturday. With the coming of electricity, the cooking range was replaced with a Devon fireplace in the living-room. This made the house a lot warmer. I used to take a metal hot-water bottle and a glass of water to bed and it was not unusual for the water in the glass to be frozen in the morning. Winters were harder in those days. Floor coverings were mainly congoleum squares with rugs – no carpets until the 1950s.

In most of the houses there were children, all about my age and we were a closely-knit community. We used to play at places such as Conygar, Dunster Beach, the football pitch near Loxhole sawmills and near Marsh Bridge. The only children's playing park in the village was at the Packhorse Bridge. I was lucky enough to have a bicycle when I was seven or eight and several of the lads learnt to ride on mine. I taught by holding the seat and running along behind to help them keep their balance.

Conygar was a place where we spent many hours. The quarry was then very active, owned by W.J. King of Bishops Lydeard and managed by Herbie Slade from Timberscombe. We kept clear of this, realising the dangers and the chance of blasting at any time, except on Saturday afternoons when work finished at noon. I remember when the machinery was brought down from the higher level to enable the quarry to be extended, probably by three times. It was closed some time in the 1960s. The road to the higher level still exists, but is overgrown. Lorries, horses and carts and steam lorries all used this steep track to take the products away. It must have been in the mid 1930s when a lady visitor was killed at the bottom of Dunster Steep by a steam lorry when I was at school. There was a little hut on the Dunster side of the quarry where I understood the explosives were kept. We kept away from that place, but it was not fenced off.

The tunnel that was supposed to run from the tower to the castle, via the Yarn Market, was not very inviting. There was a fear of bats and foxes but we as youngsters could have entered several feet at that time. During the war, perhaps in 1943, there were several military vehicles parked in the woods, for camouflage purposes I imagine.

My father always had a motor vehicle. His motor bikes were before my time but later he had several Austin 7 tourers. I passed my driving test in one at Taunton. He bought a Morgan three-wheeler in about 1938, but my mother would not ride in it, so that had to go! It was too small even for Maureen and me to sit in the 'dickey seat' at the back. We later bought a Morris 8 tourer between us for £200, but we only used it for pleasure, taxing it from April to September. There was no choice of petrol; all filling stations sold 'Pool' petrol during the war until the 1950s (providing we had coupons as rationing was still in place up to then).

The sawmill at Marsh, belonging to the Dunster Trading Company, was very busy. There was a freezing plant there where blocks of ice, approximately 6ft by 1ft by 6ins, were produced and where, on occasion, ice-cream was manufactured for sale. The ice blocks were placed in sacking material, so that they could be handled and distributed to traders and hoteliers. There were not many refrigerators or freezers at that time. The sawmills had one circular saw at first (I suppose it was driven by a turbine for water from the river fenders runs through the mill) but the main work I recall was the production of huts for Dunster Beach, all prefabricated to assemble on site. When the war came and a demand for timber, the business really took off and expanded – it acquired the neighbouring field where Bridges Mead is today. Electric high-powered band saws were installed. Chain-saws were not about then, but there was a portable mechanical saw, petrol driven, quite heavy and water cooled with a to-and-fro action. When it was set up it could be left to saw a log with a diameter of about 1ft – the process was very slow, but less hard work. Overhead gantries were erected with electric hoists and with timber not being imported the demand for home-produced timber was great. Sawdust was continually being carted to the dump (known as the ballast hole) in Sea Lane by the level crossing. It often used to catch fire and Dunster Fire Brigade spent hours trying to put it out with water from the river. This brigade was formed from the ARP and Civil Defence during the war.

The beach huts were taken over by the military during the war. The Somerset Light Infantry was

Dunster School, c.1935.

Left to right, back row: *? Prescott, Jack Heard, Peggy Prescott, Joan Gould, Robin Grant, Mabel Sage, Pauline Mumford, ?, Ivy Marchant, Vivian Sully, Leslie Griffiths, Oswald Gould, ? Pope;* centre: *Peter Tudball, ?, Ronald Mandley, Francis Sully, Josie Parkman, Margaret Burge, Kathleen Burge, Peggy Radford, Esme Ware, Mary Webber, Betty Griffiths;* front: *Maurice Case, Norman Case, Louis Pring, Ralph Strong, Raymond Davis, Alan Davis, Geoffrey Rowe, Philip Rowe, Ronald Rowe.*

Mr Flowers' friend lands on the polo ground (with Mr Luttrell's permission) in August 1937.

there initially, followed by Canadians, Americans and several British regiments. I am sure that if an invasion of England had taken place we would have been in the hot seat in this area; trenches were dug all over the place by the troops – where Bremis Road is now, all along the seashore and fields around to Blue Anchor. The summer of 1940 was very hot and I can still see the sweat on [the soldiers'] *faces now.*

All along the seashore, above the high-water mark, barbed wire was placed and on the seashore itself, pylons (wooden poles) were driven into the sand to hamper a possible landing. There were thousands of these on the beach from Blue Anchor to Minehead to Porlock Bay. However, we were still able to get on to the beach to swim.

The troops had concerts in the camp once a week and these were held where the beach shop now stands. They were open to the locals, especially the girls, and were well supported. With the occupation of the camp by the Forces many Nissen huts were assembled, and concrete pads, where the day visitors' car parking is today, were built for gun positions. Local contractors built many pillboxes, all disguised to look like ordinary houses. Some still remain today and are listed buildings.

The Hawn in my young days was always dry in the summer, and we could walk freely under the stone footbridge. I found a pheasant's nest there once – it was so arid.

Early in the war years there were troops in the Old Park with vehicles under the trees that became bogged down. It was then that I first saw a bulldozer, when hard core was spread to create makeshift roads. These roads must still exist, all overgrown with grass. The three garages belonging to the Luttrell Arms Hotel at the top of Dunster Steep were used as the officers' mess. It was probably at this time that a Bren-gun carrier was parked opposite the hotel itself, but I was never aware of it being moved. The Luttrell Arms Garage was used for making components to aid the war effort. Many women worked there on lathes, milling machines and all types of metalworking machines, probably listening to Workers' Playtime on the radio.

As a young lad I was always interested in aircraft. The air pageants, Alan Cobham's Flying Circus, were held at Twenty Acres in Sea Lane, annually on Empire Day. I remember two, probably 1936 and 1937. It was very exciting for we were able to enter the field the evening before, when most of the aircraft arrived. Attractions included the flying flea, autogyro, triplanes and biplanes. On the day itself we could not afford to go in, but with many others we stood on the hedge and looked over the canvas screens. Biplanes dropped coloured paper streamers from fairly high up and then flew through them as they descended slowly, chopping them up all the way down. Pleasure flights were on for those who could afford them, from the grass track landing strip. This popular event concluded in the early evening with parachute jumping. What a thrill!

About 1938 the airship Graf Zeppelin went up the Bristol Channel one Sunday evening when we were on our way home from a day on the beach – a lovely sight. It was flying very slowly, not making much noise and not very far out to sea. This Zeppelin was Germany's pride and joy and I can only assume now that it was on a flight from America.

Once in about 1937 a biplane crash-landed on the beach, not far from the Warren, near the golf course, and the staff of the Metropole Garage, where my father worked, retrieved the fairly intact craft before the tide came in. Mr Flowers of Northanger (a city gent) was visited by a colleague in an aeroplane one summer Sunday in 1937. It landed on the polo ground before treating Mr Flowers to a flight. In the summer of 1940, before France was invaded, four Hawker Hurricanes landed on the Minehead end of Dunster Beach one afternoon when we were at school, one on the seashore, the others on the links. They were not damaged very much, but I never knew whether anyone was injured. The tale at the time was that they had lost their way and thought they had landed on the French coast, short of fuel. Next day after school we went down to see them again, but alas they had all gone! A Spitfire crashed where Butlins is now, after it collided with its mate off Minehead seafront. I saw this from Lower Marsh and by the time I had cycled across the golf links, I was just in time to see the pilot being carried on a stretcher to an ambulance. During the collision the tail fin was damaged, resulting in a loss of control. Another time a Spitfire belly-flopped on the golf course by the beach huts, clipping the top of a bunker. I was at school when we heard the machine-gun fire when a Junkers 88 was shot down on Porlock beach. I cycled there on a Saturday afternoon and there were hundreds of others there to see it and obtain some souvenirs.

We were at choir practice when a sea mine exploded at Sampford Brett – the whole church shuddered. The Americans had a couple of Piper Cubs on the polo grounds by the pavilion. I never knew what they were about; we tried to get a flight but without success. There were barrage balloons, three at one time, one coloured green, in the field opposite the entrance to the polo ground, in the cricket field. They never went up very high, but were there for many months.

My father, Jack, my uncles and about 16 local men were all members of the Observer Corps, with a post at first near the Old Manor, then on the shoreline at the golf course, known as K2. I used to spend a lot of time there, my aircraft recognition was pretty good at that time, and I really enjoyed the hours spent there.

War was declared on a Sunday. I think that at ten years old I was too young to realise what it would mean. We must have had a radio at the time but the lines of communication were not good. People from London and the Home Counties came to the area to stay with relatives. My father's cousin's family from Folkestone came to live with us with their two young boys. My mother could not cope with the distress caused by living in rather cramped conditions, so after a couple of months they returned home. We then had soldiers and their wives and girlfriends to stay.

It was not until the bombing of such places as Birmingham, Bristol and other cities that evacuees descended upon us in great numbers. That meant great changes to us at school. Whole families from West Ham and East London who were bombed out came among us, with fresh children in our classes continually. Regent's Park Polytechnic was evacuated to Minehead, with teachers and lads billeted around the area. The Revd Mr Balleine (the vicar of Dunster) was Billeting Officer and built a bungalow in the vicarage grounds to accommodate children from an orphanage with their nuns from the Birmingham area. My parents decided to take an evacuee when a school from Horfield in Bristol was sent to West Somerset. Pupils were dropped off at the railway stations from Watchet to Dunster. Local residents went to the station to make their selection (if that's the right word). My parents asked a neighbour to collect a girl about my sister's age (11 years old), and so Beryl arrived. Later I went to live in Bristol with Beryl's family so that I could attend Bristol Secondary Technical School. Beryl remained with my family until the end of the war.

Left: *Dunster Observer Corps.* Left to right, back row: *Jack Tudball, Arthur (Birdie) Tudball, Tom Huxtable, Jim Herod, Harold Perry, Wilf Owen, Jack Griffiths, Arthur Paul, Billy Tudball, Fred Welsh;* front: *Arthur Dyer, Jack Parham, Ern Payne, Mr Mackenzie, 'Uncle' Alfie Baker, Fred Heard, Bert Hole.*

Right: *The bungalow built near the vicarage to house evacuees. After the war Mr and Mrs Lloyd lived there for many years. The bungalow was knocked down when the new vicarage was built in the 1980s.*

Chapter Thirteen

BETWEEN THE WARS: ESTATE & CASTLE

Based on the memories of Sir Walter Luttrell

In the years between the two world wars Dunster Castle estate and the castle itself, together with the Home Farm, were run as two separate enterprises. 'The Squire', Alexander Fownes Luttrell, lived at East Quantoxhead and ran the estate with its numerous farms and other properties in Dunster, Minehead and the surrounding villages. His son, Geoffrey Fownes Luttrell, lived with his family at the castle and ran the Home Farm.

Sir Walter Luttrell recalls that the number of people working on the castle estate was at its peak when he was about five years old. Development in both Minehead and Alcombe was still going on, and the family were responsible for the maintenance of several streets, sewers and water supplies, so there were two steamrollers down in the yard and several lorries with their attendant crews. The steamrollers were not madly popular with his mother, as at children's parties at the castle everyone wanted to climb on them in preference to taking part in a treasure hunt or similar entertainment that she had carefully planned. 'I fear the result was often our guests' return to their respective mothers in clothes less pristine than when they had arrived.'

Walter Luttrell on the beach at Blue Anchor, c.1922.

Working on the estate was a forestry gang of six or seven under the Head Forester, Cuthill, a somewhat excitable Scot with a passion for cricket. The estate sawmill at Loxhole had a staff of three or four plus another man whose time was largely spent in the tree nursery, which was on the right over the packhorse bridge.

Mr Simpson, the Clerk of Works, headed the maintenance staff which consisted of the house carpenter (Webber) and his 'boy', the joiner-cum-wheelwright (Quick), the plumber (Timewell) and his mate and three or four others including the two invaluable Griffiths brothers who found blocked drains with unerring accuracy. All these were under the command of the estate agent, Mr Willie Mackenzie – a bachelor who for many years lodged at Lock's Café in the High Street – then about the only tea shop in Dunster! Subsequently he married Mrs Luttrell's secretary and they lived at the bottom of Castle Steep. The estate office was in the castle gatehouse and here the agent was assisted by an accountant, Morris, whose superb calligraphy will undoubtedly continue to impress future researchers into the more recent account books and records of the estate. There was also a young clerk, usually only a temporary member of the staff who was learning estate agency. All in all the weekly pay parade on Saturday mornings at the tithe barn saw a muster of about 25.

In addition the Home Farm employed two cowmen for the Jersey herd, a shepherd and four carters. The dairy was run by the Clatworthy family to produce butter and scalded cream both for the house and for much-demanded local sale, and woe betide any guest at the castle who unwittingly admired it as 'Devonshire' cream.

The laundry, down at Marsh, was run by two sisters, the Miss Dyers, who, Sir Walter recalls, 'in later years never seemed put out however filthy my white breeches were – beagling, hunting or polo.'

The 'household staff' were employed by Mr and Mrs Geoffrey Luttrell and were quite separate from

Between the Wars

Left: *Nursemaids at the castle, 1921. Edith Parker, on the right, looked after the young Walter.*

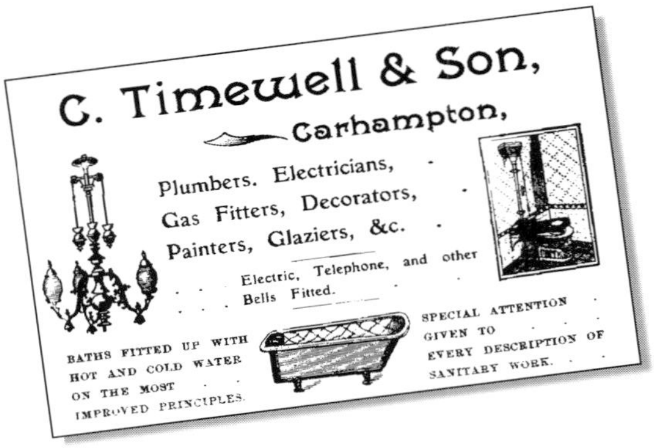

DUNSTER CASTLE
will be OPEN to the PUBLIC:—

June .... Wednesdays and Thursdays
July, August, September
Tuesdays, Wednesdays and Thursdays
Easter, Spring and August Bank Holiday Monday
} 10.15 a.m. to 12.40 p.m. and 2.15 p.m. to 4.40 p.m.

WINTER SEASON:
October to May ..... Wednesday Afternoons only } 2.15 p.m. to 3.30 p.m.

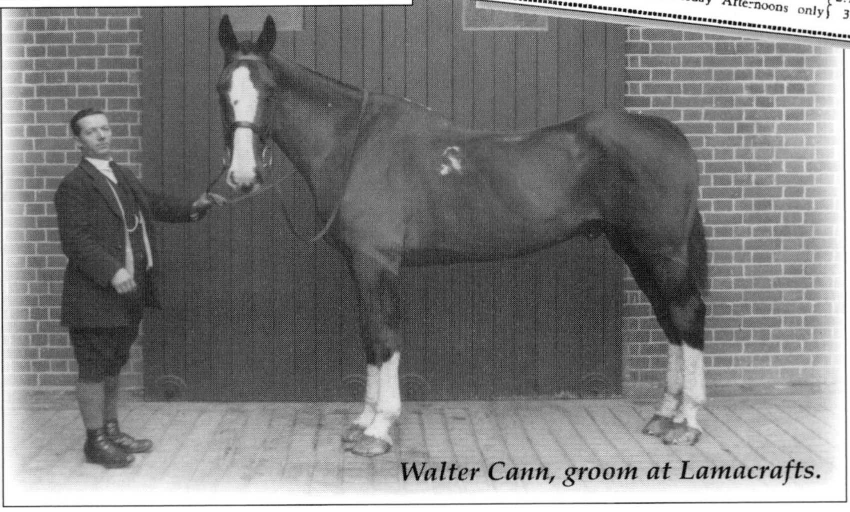

Walter Cann, groom at Lamacrafts.

Right: *Staff at the dairy in later years. Mr Boyles, Mr Gillard and Joyce Downs. Steve Bowden remembers going to fetch the milk each day from the dairy during the 1940s. He also recalls that if the cap of the metal milkcan was a tight enough fit you could safely whirl the can around... If not, disaster!*

the estate people employed by the Squire. In the early 1930s there was a butler (Patfield), a footman (George Griffiths), a pantry boy, a cook (Mrs Jenkins) plus a kitchen maid and scullery maid. 'Upstairs' there was Lily Parkman as head housemaid with two under-housemaids – often young Welsh girls who never seemed to stay very long as 'surprise pregnancy' appeared to be a fairly regular impediment to continuous employment, remembers Sir Walter.

Outside staff consisted of Frank Swain, the chauffeur, Hardwick, head gardener for many years, with two under-gardeners in the kitchen garden. Charlie Thrush looked after the front lawn, the terrace and the bowling green – having by then progressed, with considerable trepidation, from a pony-pulled mower to a temperamental Atco. He had been at the castle since leaving school, when Sir Walter's great-grandmother was in residence:

She was a formidable lady who made a habit of collecting all the bits left over after breakfast – toast, porridge, etc. and throwing them out of the dining-room window, calling out, 'Birdie, Birdie'. One morning soon after Charlie started work he was unfortunately passing directly under the window and the birds' rations scored a direct hit. His exclamation of surprise caused my great-grandmother to look down.

'What's your name, boy?'
'Thrush, madam.'
'Don't be so impertinent!' and she slammed the window.

Later Tom and Jim Copp looked after an extra bit of vegetable garden to the west of the mill.

When Mr and Mrs Luttrell first came to Dunster the stables were not used. Mrs Luttrell kept her horse at livery with Major Rose in Minehead, while Edgar Lamacraft looked after Sir Walter's early mounts in his West Street stables. Then the stables at the castle were 'renovated' by turning some of the old stalls into boxes where the hunters – and later the polo ponies – were looked after by Mason, the head groom, and a young 'strapper'.

In the earliest days Mr Luttrell had one gamekeeper (Harry Flapman), but later he employed a head keeper (Jackson) and two beat-keepers – Joyce at Boniton and another at Rodhuish. Harry Hole from Carhampton looked after the ferrets and was always on hand to help Jackson on the rearing field.

Sir Walter has vivid memories of Christmas at the castle:

At Christmas all the employees met together – firstly for a ritual distribution of presents in the Morning Room by Mother. A jersey each for the men, plus a cigar or cigarettes from Father, and a Christmas pudding, sweets, biscuits, etc. for the wives according to the size and ages of their families.

Then on Christmas Day evening there was the staff party and Christmas dinner in the servants' hall, when Father carved the turkey (usually two monsters were required) and I helped to dish it around to everyone.

As a family we very much followed tradition. A Christmas tree at the far end of the hall, an ashen faggot in the fireplace and a snapdragon on the table – all on Christmas Eve before the arrival of the church choir to sing carols in the hall. My father invariably produced an exceedingly powerful hot red wine punch after the singing, and succeeding vicars often remarked on the 'extra power and individuality' of various members of their choir at the Midnight Service which immediately followed this visit to the castle. I used to enjoy watching for the occasional 'lurch' of a chorister during their procession up the aisle!

Two other annual events stand out in those pre-war days. First, the schoolchildren's Christmas party which was held in the Tenants' Hall. Mr and Mrs Luttrell took particular trouble over this and unfailingly provided a tremendous spread together with entertainment – often Harold Perry, the tailor in Dunster, who was a marvellous professional conjuror – and small presents for everyone, crackers and so on.

The other great event was the Tenants' Audit Dinner held, obviously, in the Tenants' Hall and presided over by Mr Alexander Luttrell. It coincided with the payment of rents by the farm tenants of the estate at Michaelmas and some 30 men sat down to a traditional lunch, which sometimes ended with a few words from 'The Squire' about any particular agricultural subject likely to affect the estate's farms or smallholdings. Sir Walter was introduced to this assembly at a very early age when he distinguished himself by ferociously tugging at the beard of the senior tenant, Mr Case, in an effort to determine whether it was real! Although 'The Squire' was a strict teetotaller himself he insisted that the wine – or cider or beer – should flow freely, and Sir Walter believes that present-day breathalysers would have had a bonanza had they been in operation in the village when some of the guests departed homewards.

During the second half of the 1930s, Mr and Mrs Luttrell entertained extensively. In the winter it was mostly shooting parties, and in the summer polo was the main attraction for guests. Geoffrey Luttrell was a superb shot and unlike his father, wife and elder son was not particularly keen on horse or hound. Although he was quite indifferent to the present-day obsession with numbers of pheasants killed he did insist on every drive being organised to produce the highest and most difficult birds possible – and this he achieved on three of the separate beats: Carhampton, the Oak coverts at Rodhuish and the Big Woods around Broadwood Farm, where several of the drives were almost legendary. Equally well known amongst their friends were Mrs Luttrell's shooting lunches, brought out to whichever beat was being shot that day.

The Tenants' Dinner, 1933.
Included in the back row: *Adams, Baker (Briddicott), ?, Morris (office), O'Shea (office), W. Webber (Minehead), Phillips, Prout, M. Thomas, Adams (Ash), Patfield (butler);*
third row: *Baker (Briddicott), T. Tapp (Alcombe), S.G. Burgess (Dunster), Eames, ?, W. Yeandle, Simpson, ? Vaulter (Broadwood cottage), Bond, King, J.H. Burnell (Aller), ?;*
second row: *? Norman (Broadwood), Cuthill, Case, R.K. Ridler (Periton), Alexander Fownes Luttrell, Watts, Mackenzie, Hagley (Combe), ?, ?, F. Thomas;*
front: *Eames (office), ? Case (Roadwater), N. Hepper, Passmore, D. Hepper, F. Mathews (Minehead).*

Sir Walter recalls that in those days he had very little interest in shooting; both he and his mother were far keener on hunting:

We each had good horses and hunted regularly with the West Somerset, who in those days also covered the country now hunted by the West Somerset Vale. We quite often went out with the Minehead Harriers if the foxhounds were at the far eastern side of the country. We never had a horsebox and always hacked to any meet – and home again at the end of the day. Neither of us were particularly keen on staghunting, although if we had guests staying who wanted to have a day with the Devon and Somerset I would usually go with them.

My love of hunting involved me at a very early age with what were known as The Castle Rabbit Hounds – a motley collection of terriers, spaniels and all sorts, with which three or four of us used to chase rabbits about in the Deer Park, on Grabbist or around the Tor. From this 'pack' I was allowed to progress to my own pack of beagles, with which I had tremendous fun for five seasons until the war. In spite of the number of Hunts operating in this area, the Dunster Castle Beagles became very popular, and at our Boxing Day meet in the village in 1937 someone standing at the Luttrell Arms corner counted 318 people following us down to the marshes when we moved off.

Lawn meet at the castle, c.1930.
Left to right: *Alexander Fownes Luttrell, Geoffrey Fownes Luttrell, H. Worral, Lady Boles, Mrs Alys Luttrell, Walter Luttrell and Sir Dennis Boles MFH. Bernard is in the foreground.*

The main social event of the summer was undoubtedly Dunster Show. Although there were always very popular classes for cattle and sheep, it was, perhaps, predominantly a horse show – largely owing to the number of high-class hunters and polo ponies which were 'visiting' at the time. But as well as all the varied classes for riding horses, those for draught-horses proved the most popular with the public. It was a marvellous sight to see the different types being shown in well-filled classes – some in their owners' wagons, others 'in hand' – the mares often with foals at foot. There were wonderful horse brasses, studded harness straps, manes and tails plaited with coloured ribbons, and with coats 'strapped' until their huge bodies looked as if they could have been varnished. This all entailed a great deal of work on the part of their respective carters, all of which was carried out in their own time, after they finished work at 5p.m., for several evenings before the show.

Left: *Walter Luttrell with his beagles at a meet at Dunster Station, 1936.*

Moving off towards the marshes, 1936.

Sir Walter remembers that there was intense rivalry at home between the farm and forestry shire horses belonging to the estate, and those which belonged to his father and which were used by his little company – the onetime Dunster Trading & Transport Company. 'I never knew whether it was chance or diplomacy on the part of successive judges, but it seemed that each of the rivals scored over the other in alternate years.'

The show of 1939 clearly stands out in Sir Walter's memory:

I was showing one of my horses for the first time in the heavyweight hunter class. He had never been in a show ring before, but behaved beautifully and attracted the early attention of the two judges. The one to ride him first was Captain 'Tiddley' Lucas – a very well known judge but an extremely small man (hence his nickname) – who was never particularly fond of heavyweight horses. I had to give him a strong leg-up into the saddle (Cashbox being 17.2hh) and no sooner had he landed than Cashbox decided to put in a gigantic buck which almost deposited Captain Lucas back into my arms. Needless to say, he was not amused. However his fellow judge had a beautiful ride on my horse, over-ruled Lucas's objections, and Cashbox received the Class Winner's blue rosette.

But shortly after that the commentator announced over the public address system that Germany had invaded Poland – so war was inevitable. Everyone packed up and hurried home to deal with the 'blacking out' and other mandatory preparations. A friend from Ireland was staying with me and the moment we got up to the house from the stables, Father issued us with a couple of brushes and gallons of black paint and told us to black out the uncurtained windows: the tower stair-case, kitchen quarters, passages and so on. I don't know what he thought was going to happen that night but I know he wouldn't even let me change out of my breeches and boots before we set to work. I never knew before how many bits of plain glass there were in even the part of the house we were using!

However, we completed our task, even though one result was a pair of breeches ruined by black paint, although miraculously the boots came through unscathed. But it did not really matter as those particular 'best' breeches would not be needed again for six years – by which time they were hopelessly out of fashion anyway.

Dunster Trading & Transport Company

Started by Mr Geoffrey Luttrell in the 1920s, the company's activities included the import of coal, the construction of the first chalets for Dunster Beach and the manufacture of ice, cider and meat pies using local produce. A camping ground was provided at Blue Anchor around 1936. Perhaps the most exciting venture was the building of Minehead Swimming Pool with its Olympic-sized pool filled with sea water, and its restaurant with a resident orchestra. Sadly the problems caused by the salt water eventually made the project economically unviable.

Jack Haydon worked for Dunster Trading Company for a while in the early years:

In those days we started work at 6.30a.m. My first job was to clean the offices at the entrance to the castle from High Street. Mr Fred Burt was Manager. Then we had to do any sort of jobs. They used to keep a lot of pigs, which they killed and made bacon and hams. Miss Amelia Payne of West Street had an open fire and used to smoke some of the hams. They had salterns made on the left-hand side of the castle gatehouse and we used to salt the sides of bacon and hams and sweet pickle them; old William Thrush was in charge. Sometimes I drove a horse and cart, hauling hard core for roads in Minehead from Hopcott Quarry. Then there was the cider business, we used to make hogsheads of cider at Kitswall Farm and take them back to the stables at the castle and then bottle a lot to send away. Chopping sticks, mostly faggot wood, for the offices and castle for lighting fires used to take some time. Jim Edwards was bailiff for the old squire at the time and Jim Tame and Ned Gillard milked the cows and looked after the stock. Fred Tapp was a farm hand and Bill Gay a shepherd.

Ike Farmer* (left) *and Jack Griffiths in the cab of YA599 in the late 1920s. On the side is painted G.F. Luttrell, Dunster.

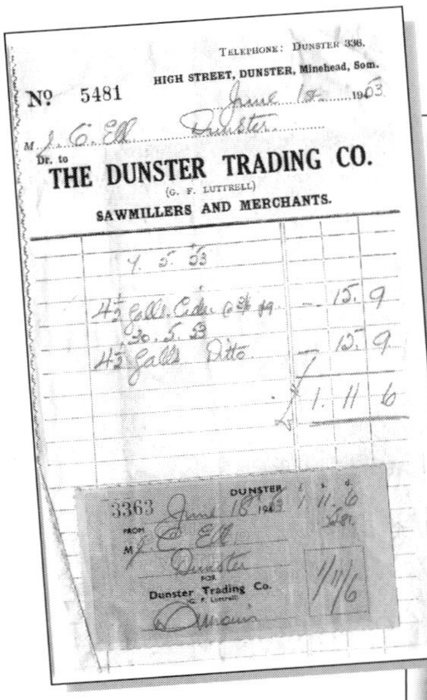

A Trading Company bill.

John Miles outside the butcher's shop in Carhampton with a prize bull, reared for the Prince of Wales, and bought at Smithfield Market by Mr Luttrell for slaughter and sale.

Chapter Fourteen

POLO BETWEEN THE WARS

The West Somerset Polo Grounds on Dunster Castle Lawns c.1929.

Polo was established in West Somerset in 1904 when the West Somerset Polo Club was founded with nine or ten playing members and Mr J.P. Goddard as the first Hon. Secretary. For the first six years of its life the club played on a field at New Bridge near Porlock. Then, in 1910, under a new Secretary, Major J. Vere Foster, the club began to expand and negotiations with Mr Alexander Luttrell led to the establishment of a new playing ground on Dunster Castle Lawns. A small pavilion was built together with accommodation for the ponies. During the First World War play was suspended but in 1920 the club was reopened and began to go from strength to strength with teams from the Army and many well-known players taking part in the autumn tournament including, in 1923, the Rt Hon. Winston Churchill. The quality of play began to attract great crowds to the events and in 1924 a second playing ground was opened adjacent to the first.

The year 1925 marked the first visit of the Indian polo teams that were to cause so much interest and excitement and become the stuff of many local people's memories. In that year the Jodhpur Polo Team stayed in the area for two months and the Maharajah of Jodhpur enjoyed himself so much that he presented the club with a new pavilion.

During the later 1930s Sir Walter Luttrell had the opportunity of playing polo on occasion with some of the players with the highest handicaps in the country. He recalls his memories of those days:

It is hard now to picture the number of horses that were stabled in the area around Dunster during the summers of the 1930s. At the height of the polo season – late August and early September when visiting teams arrived after the Hurlingham and Ranelagh tournaments had finished – it would have been impossible to find room for a Shetland pony in Dunster,

1920s Polo

A parade of polo ponies, 2 May 1925.

The Jodhpur team, August 1925.

The New Pavilion presented to the club by the Maharajah of Jodhpur in 1925.

Left: *The president of the West Somerset Polo Club (Mr R.B. Magor) and some of the players, 1930.*

Above: *People crowded to view the polo in the 1930s.*

Below: *Winners of the West Somerset Senior Polo Cup, 1932.*

Timberscombe or Minehead. In addition to the numerous strings of polo ponies which arrived by special train to Dunster Station, there was the annual invasion of people bringing their hunters down from up country to staghunt, with the idea of getting them fit for the coming foxhunting season. The fact that far from getting fit, the majority of these lovely thoroughbreds either 'blew up' negotiating Exmoor's steeper combes, or lamed themselves on the stony tracks, never appeared to deter their owners from returning the next summer.

But polo was the main attraction of the pre-war summers. Geologists tell us that when the Ice-Age glaciers on Exmoor melted, they carved out the Avill Valley until they met the Castle Tor, split on either side and left a bed of alluvial gravel beneath what are now the Higher Lawns and the old Polo Ground. This resulted in superb drainage beneath the ancient turf – which had never been ploughed until the Second World War – so that polo could be played within half an hour of the heaviest summer thunderstorm. This fact made our club the envy of every polo club in Britain and was one of the features that originally attracted the crack regimental and civilian teams to our spring and so-called autumn tournaments. During the latter, play took place – often on both grounds simultaneously – on three and sometimes four afternoons a week and matches attracted large numbers of spectators. Among the many famous teams that played at Dunster (including both Service and civilian) by far the most colourful were those of the Maharajahs of Jodhpur and Jaipur. I cannot remember very much about Jodhpur's visit

Schooling and conditioning ponies from Jodhpur on Minehead sands.

except for the fact that he was an extremely short man. He drove a large old-fashioned Rolls Royce, which he was only able to navigate if he peered through the gap between the top of the dashboard and the top rim of the steering wheel. Early one morning he was driving into Minehead in order to watch some of his ponies exercising on the beach when he met the local bobby on his bicycle. As far as the constable could see, here was a driverless runaway car careering down Tregonwell Road, so he turned and pedalled after it, anticipating a mighty crash as it piled up against the wall across the Avenue. But to his amazement, the car turned right of its own accord, right again and pulled up by the old slipway. Rumour has it that he pedalled straight back to the police station and signed the Pledge!

The Maharajah of Jaipur brought his famous Indian team to play at Dunster on two occasions. On the second he stayed with us at the castle and stabled his ponies down below. Two things stand out in my memory about his week-long visit. After any dinner party hosted by my parents he invited our guests to visit the stables, which of course everyone wanted to do. So we would all descend the Steep – in full evening rig with the ladies having great difficulty in either borrowed slippers or their own high heels – and then walk along the lines of ponies in their stalls. Although there was ample comfortable accommodation above the stables for the sices (grooms) they steadfastly refused to use it and each sice slept curled up under his pony's manger – a wonderful sight.

The Maharajah brought his own Indian staff with him, headed by his personal bearer or major domo – a magnificent bearded Sikh of 6ft 2ins. He was always superbly dressed in white jodhpur breeches, white jacket and a gloriously coloured silk turban. He was a delightful man who got on extremely well with our own staff.

On one occasion the Maharajah asked my mother whether, for a forthcoming lunch party, she would like his cook to prepare a proper Indian curry. She was delighted to accept. After several telephone calls to different shops in Soho, a parcel of various ingredients arrived by train at Dunster Station and the cook duly got to work. The result was terrific to say the least. However, the 'joyous anticipation' on the part of our guests turned to agonised gasps at the first incautious mouthfuls. It was touch and go whether the fire brigade would have to be summoned! Father always said it was the most expensive lunch party for which he provided the wine because the butler, Patfield, was forced to make almost continuous trips down to the cellar for reinforcements.

Another incident of that visit was when Jaipur's own favourite pony, a chestnut mare called Princess which was subject to previously incurable outbreaks of warts, suddenly developed a bunch exactly under her girth so that of course she could not be ridden. Jaipur was terribly upset as in spite of the efforts of the best vets in India and England these outbreaks could never be cured and often remained for two or three months before receding. So my mother suggested that he might like to ask Mr Ayres to charm this new bunch of warts away. Mr Ayres was a well-known and enormously successful 'charmer-cum-healer' who lived in West Street and had on several occasions produced instant cures for milk fever in our cows and stubborn lameness in a cart-horse.

Not surprisingly, the Maharajah agreed at once and Mr Ayres was asked to come up to the stables to see the pony. However the 'house telephone' from the stables soon rang with the head sice saying that Ayres would not let him go into Princess's box with him, and he would not let Ayres go in alone. However, when he learned that Ayres had no drugs, ointments or any medications, just his Bible, Jaipur instructed his head man to allow Ayres to enter the box alone. I gather he was only in there about five minutes. Almost immediately the warts started to shrivel; by that afternoon they had disappeared, and the following day Jaipur was able to ride Princess in the finals of the West Somerset Cup. We learned two years later that no more warts had appeared anywhere on that pony. Jaipur's efforts to reward Mr Ayres with either money or a present were strenuously rejected – in fact I believe he became very angry and told the Maharajah that if he had thought he was going to be offered payment of any sort for his services he would not have gone near the pony.

I had the enormous good luck to start playing polo two seasons before the Second World War broke out and on occasion, when one of the crack teams happened to be short of a member for some game, they were kind enough to invite me to play for them as No.1 (the least-skilled member of a side). As such, every now and then I found myself playing with three other men who were often amongst the highest-handicapped players in the country. This, of course, was a marvellous experience!

Among the world famous teams that played at Dunster was Keith Rouse's 'Jaguars' which contained the only two '10 handicap' players in England at that time – Hesky Hughes and Gerald Balding. But there were also many other well-known players taking part in the tournament, such as the film star Leslie Howard. He was an enthusiastic player, but was hampered by very poor eyesight and considerable lack of skill as a rider! However, his presence always produced a queue of fans after a match asking him to autograph used polo balls for them.

When not actually down on the Polo Ground we sometimes used to watch games from the upstairs windows, where one got a marvellous bird's eye view of proceedings. As sound rises far more clearly than it spreads horizontally, one was treated in full to the language for which polo is renowned. In fact I found I had no new words to learn from the Army when I finally joined my Regiment!

Winning Teams

Polo on the Lawns was always an exciting spectacle.

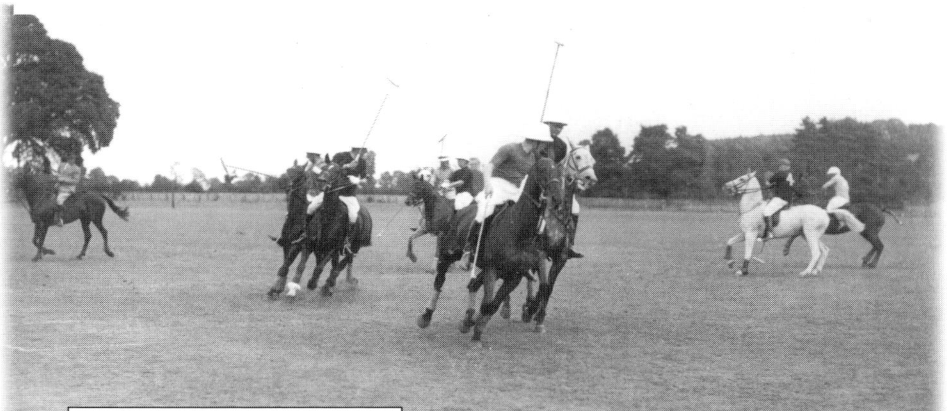

A winning combination, 1937.

Walter Luttrell receives the cup from Diana Lister.

Below: *A. Tighe, Alex Phillipi, Walter Luttrell and Gerald Balding.*

Below, left: *An unidentified but successful women's team photographed by Kingsley Taylor in July 1938.*

The Foresters' Arms, then known as the Foresters Hotel, in the 1920s. This was surely an advertising card designed to attract the hunting and polo fraternity.

Mrs Petford, daughter of Edgar Dyer the saddler, recalled that polo often brought extra revenue to the village:

The Luttrell Arms Hotel had adequate stabling for players from the Argentine and the players would stay at the hotel. (When the polo ceased the stables were converted into sleeping-quarters for the hotel staff.) My father was at hand to do bridle repairs and so on and would also rebind the handles of the polo sticks. Alfred Hole (cabinet-maker) would shorten old sticks so that the young village boys could play polo on their bicycles in the playing field.

She also remembered that between the chukkas the spectators would take part in 'treading'. They would rush on to the pitch and tread in the turf that had been kicked up by the horses.

The Second World War brought an end to polo in Dunster. After the war those heady days of the 1920s and '30s were never regained.

Chapter Fifteen

Growing Things

At a meeting held at the Luttrell Arms Hotel in May 1869, the great and the good of Dunster and the area round about agreed to establish a Horticultural Society. Its aim was to encourage cottagers to exhibit flowers, fruit and vegetables and receive prizes, thus discouraging them from drinking, gambling and fighting. It was intended that these new pastimes should make the population happier and richer.

The first show was held on Dunster Lawns on Thursday 26 August 1869. The town itself was en fête with arches of evergreens and handmade flowers strung across the High Street bearing inscriptions such as 'Welcome'; 'Unity, Peace and Concord' as well as 'Success to our Venture'. The church bells were rung and very little business was done that day. In the marquee there was a variety of wonderful displays of hothouse flowers and fruit provided by gentlemen's gardeners in addition to cottagers' exhibits. Mr Summerhayes' band from Taunton played, refreshments were provided by

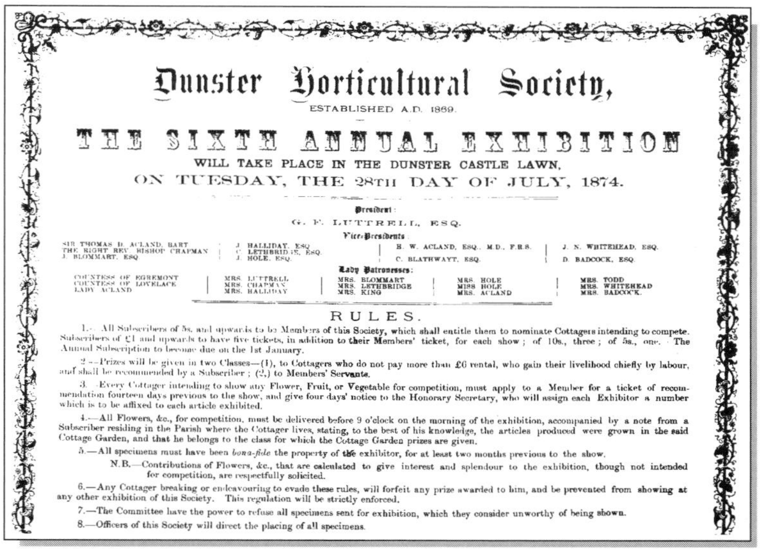

Dunster Horticultural Society,

ESTABLISHED A.D. 1869.

THE SIXTH ANNUAL EXHIBITION

WILL TAKE PLACE IN THE DUNSTER CASTLE LAWN,

ON TUESDAY, THE 28TH DAY OF JULY, 1874.

President:

G. F. LUTTRELL, ESQ.

Vice-Presidents:

SIR THOMAS D. ACLAND, BART | J. HALLIDAY, ESQ. | H. W. ACLAND, ESQ., M.D., F.R.S. | J. N. WHITEHEAD, ESQ.
THE RIGHT REV. BISHOP CHAPMAN | C. LETHBRIDGE, ESQ. | C. BLATHWAYT, ESQ. | D. BADCOCK, ESQ.
J. BLOMMART, ESQ. | J. HOLE, ESQ.

Lady Patronesses:

COUNTESS OF EGREMONT | MRS. LUTTRELL | MRS. BLOMMART | MRS. HOLE | MRS. TODD
COUNTESS OF LOVELACE | MRS. CHAPMAN | MRS. LETHBRIDGE | MISS HOLE | MRS. WHITEHEAD
LADY ACLAND | MRS. HALLIDAY | MRS. KING | MRS. ACLAND | MRS. BADCOCK.

RULES.

1.—All Subscribers of 5s. and upwards to be Members of this Society, which shall entitle them to nominate Cottagers intending to compete. Subscribers of £1 and upwards to have five tickets, in addition to their Members' ticket, for each show; of 10s., three; of 5s., one. The Annual Subscription to become due on the 1st January.

2.—Prizes will be given in two Classes—(1), to Cottagers who do not pay more than £6 rental, who gain their livelihood chiefly by labour, and shall be recommended by a Subscriber; (2,) to Members' Servants.

3.—Every Cottager intending to show any Flower, Fruit, or Vegetable for competition, must apply to a Member for a ticket of recommendation fourteen days previous to the show, and give four days' notice to the Honorary Secretary, who will assign each Exhibitor a number which is to be affixed to each article exhibited.

4.—All Flowers, &c., for competition, must be delivered before 9 o'clock on the morning of the exhibition, accompanied by a note from a Subscriber residing in the Parish where the Cottager lives, stating, to the best of his knowledge, the articles produced were grown in the said Cottage Garden, and that he belongs to the class for which the Cottage Garden prizes are given.

5.—All specimens must have been *bona-fide* the property of the exhibitor, for at least two months previous to the show.

N.B.—Contributions of Flowers, &c., that are calculated to give interest and splendour to the exhibition, though not intended for competition, are respectfully solicited.

6.—Any Cottager breaking or endeavouring to evade these rules, will forfeit any prize awarded to him, and be prevented from showing at any other exhibition of this Society. This regulation will be strictly enforced.

7.—The Committee have the power to refuse all specimens sent for exhibition, which they consider unworthy of being shown.

8.—Officers of this Society will direct the placing of all specimens.

Poster advertising a show, c.1870.

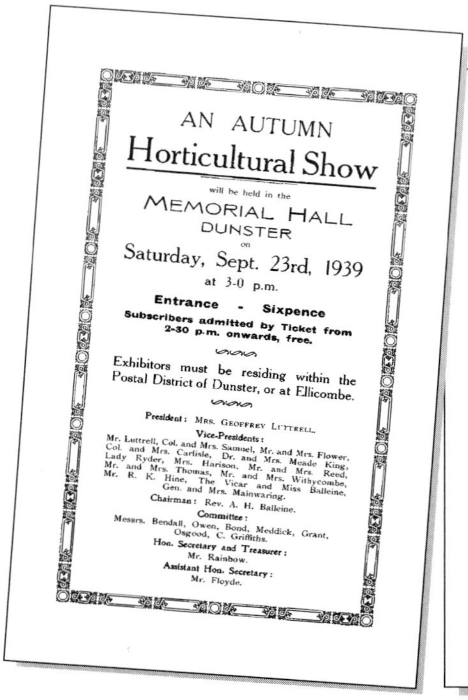

AN AUTUMN

Horticultural Show

will be held in the

MEMORIAL HALL

DUNSTER

on

Saturday, Sept. 23rd, 1939

at 3-0 p.m.

Entrance - Sixpence

Subscribers admitted by Ticket from 2-30 p.m. onwards, free.

Exhibitors must be residing within the Postal District of Dunster, or at Ellicombe.

President: Mrs. Geoffrey Luttrell.

Vice-Presidents:

Mr. Luttrell, Col. and Mrs. Samuel, Mr. and Mrs. Flower, Col. and Mrs. Carlisle, Dr. and Mrs. Meade King, Lady Ryder, Mrs. Harison, Mr. and Mrs. Reed, Mr. and Mrs. Thomas, Mr. and Mrs. Withycombe, Mr. R. K. Hine, The Vicar and Miss Balleine, Gen. and Mrs. Mainwaring.

Chairman: Rev. A. H. Balleine.

Committee:

Messrs. Bendall, Owen, Bond, Meddick, Grant, Osgood, C. Griffiths.

Hon. Secretary and Treasurer:

Mr. Rainbow.

Assistant Hon. Secretary:

Mr. Floyde.

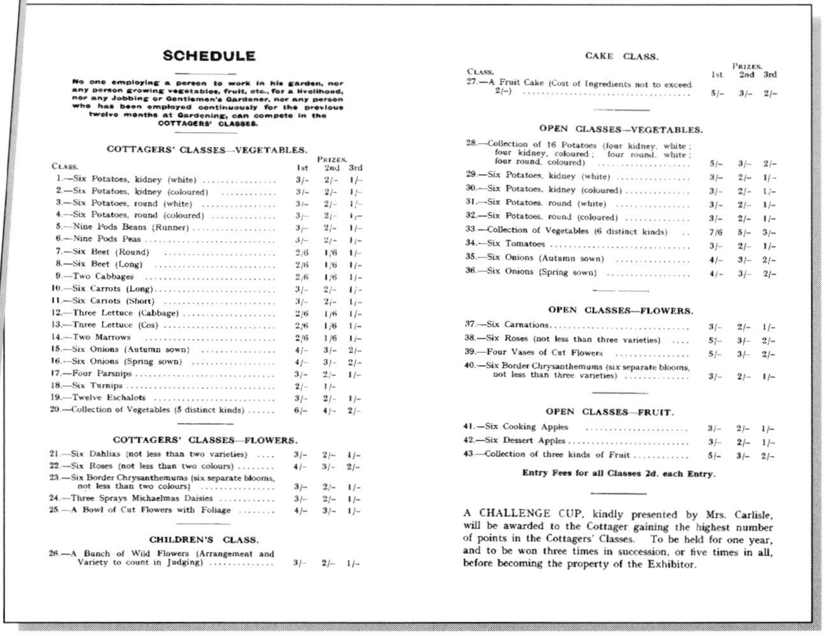

SCHEDULE

No one employing a person to work in his garden, nor any person growing vegetables, fruit, etc., for a livelihood, nor any Jobbing or Gentlemen's Gardener, nor any person who has been employed continuously for the previous twelve months at Gardening, can compete in the COTTAGERS' CLASSES.

COTTAGERS' CLASSES—VEGETABLES.

Class.	Prizes. 1st	2nd	3rd
1.—Six Potatoes, kidney (white)	3/-	2/-	1/-
2.—Six Potatoes, kidney (coloured)	3/-	2/-	1/-
3.—Six Potatoes, round (white)	3/-	2/-	1/-
4.—Six Potatoes, round (coloured)	3/-	2/-	1/-
5.—Nine Pods Beans (Runner)	3/-	2/-	1/-
6.—Nine Pods Peas	3/-	2/-	1/-
7.—Six Beet (Round)	2/6	1/6	1/-
8.—Six Beet (Long)	2/6	1/6	1/-
9.—Two Cabbages	2/6	1/6	1/-
10.—Six Carrots (Long)	3/-	2/-	1/-
11.—Six Carrots (Short)	3/-	2/-	1/-
12.—Three Lettuce (Cabbage)	2/6	1/6	1/-
13.—Three Lettuce (Cos)	2/6	1/6	1/-
14.—Two Marrows	2/6	1/6	1/-
15.—Six Onions (Autumn sown)	4/-	3/-	2/-
16.—Six Onions (Spring sown)	4/-	3/-	2/-
17.—Four Parsnips	3/-	2/-	1/-
18.—Six Turnips	2/-	1/-	
19.—Twelve Eschalots	3/-	2/-	1/-
20.—Collection of Vegetables (5 distinct kinds)	6/-	4/-	2/-

COTTAGERS' CLASSES—FLOWERS.

21.—Six Dahlias (not less than two varieties)	3/-	2/-	1/-
22.—Six Roses (not less than two colours)	4/-	3/-	2/-
23.—Six Border Chrysanthemums (six separate blooms, not less than two colours)	3/-	2/-	1/-
24.—Three Sprays Michaelmas Daisies	3/-	2/-	1/-
25.—A Bowl of Cut Flowers with Foliage	4/-	3/-	1/-

CHILDREN'S CLASS.

26.—A Bunch of Wild Flowers (Arrangement and Variety to count in Judging)	3/-	2/-	1/-

CAKE CLASS.

Class.	Prizes. 1st	2nd	3rd
27.—A Fruit Cake (Cost of Ingredients not to exceed 2/-)	5/-	3/-	2/-

OPEN CLASSES—VEGETABLES.

28.—Collection of 16 Potatoes (four kidney, white; four kidney, coloured; four round, white; four round, coloured)	5/-	3/-	2/-
29.—Six Potatoes, kidney (white)	3/-	2/-	1/-
30.—Six Potatoes, kidney (coloured)	3/-	2/-	1/-
31.—Six Potatoes, round (white)	3/-	2/-	1/-
32.—Six Potatoes, round (coloured)	3/-	2/-	1/-
33.—Collection of Vegetables (6 distinct kinds)	7/6	5/-	3/-
34.—Six Tomatoes	3/-	2/-	1/-
35.—Six Onions (Autumn sown)	4/-	3/-	2/-
36.—Six Onions (Spring sown)	4/-	3/-	2/-

OPEN CLASSES—FLOWERS.

37.—Six Carnations	3/-	2/-	1/-
38.—Six Roses (not less than three varieties)	5/-	3/-	2/-
39.—Four Vases of Cut Flowers	5/-	3/-	2/-
40.—Six Border Chrysanthemums (six separate blooms, not less than three varieties)	3/-	2/-	1/-

OPEN CLASSES—FRUIT.

41.—Six Cooking Apples	3/-	2/-	1/-
42.—Six Dessert Apples	3/-	2/-	1/-
43.—Collection of three kinds of Fruit	5/-	3/-	2/-

Entry Fees for all Classes 2d. each Entry.

A CHALLENGE CUP, kindly presented by Mrs. Carlisle, will be awarded to the Cottager gaining the highest number of points in the Cottagers' Classes. To be held for one year, and to be won three times in succession, or five times in all, before becoming the property of the Exhibitor.

Dunster Horticultural Society and Show.

Jim Griffiths, Karl Meddick, Wendy Ayres and Wes Gould with their prize exhibits at Dunster Flower Show, 1990.

DUNSTER HORTICULTURAL SOCIETY

Annual Flower Show
to be held in the
DUNSTER MEMORIAL HALL
on SATURDAY, 4th AUGUST 2001
Doors open at 2.15pm Admission 40p

President: J. Luttrell, Esq.
Hon. Vice - President: Mr. R. Harborne
Chairman: Mr. R. Nicholson F.R.C.S
Vice - Chairman: Mrs. M. Cameron
Treasurer: Mrs. B. Bale
1 Conygar House, The Ball, Dunster
Secretary: Mr. J. Melbourne
Wolverton Cottage, 2 Park Street, Dunster 821109

Committee:
Mesdames M. Gould, R. Fox, J. Nicholson, B. Priddle, J. Vaulter.
Messrs. R. Grant, R. Hutchings, P. Stanford.

Judges:
Mesdames M. Bawden, J. Collins, E. Picton. Messrs. J. Bracey, G. Holt, K. Durman.

POINTS AWARDS

Perpetual Cups to be held for one year.
THE MEDDICK CUP (in Memory of Ken Meddick) for the highest points in class 1-4 inclusive.
PRODUCE CUP for the exhibitor with the highest points in classes 1-26
CORONATION CHALLENGE CUP for the highest number of points in the Fruit and Vegetable Classes.
FOLJAMBE CUP for the highest points in the flower section.
W. FROST CUP for the highest points in the Dahlia classes.
THE DURRANT ROSE CUP for the highest points in Classes 36, 37 & 38.
VICE - PRESIDENT'S ROSE BOWL for the highest points in the flower and pot plant classes.
THE LUTTRELL CUP for the second highest points in the flower and pot plant classes.
THE HORNBY TROPHY for the highest points in the homecraft section.
THE LADIES' CHALLENGE CUP for the second highest points in the homecraft section.
THE PRIDDLE SALVER for most points when not having previously won a trophy in homecraft section.
THE VAULTER CUP for the child with highest points in homecraft section.
THE JULIAN LUTTRELL CUP for the highest points in the Children's classes.
THE WILLIS CUP for the highest points in pot plants.
B. R. GRIFFITHS CUP (donated by Mr. J. Griffiths) for the NOVICE with the most points in classes 1 - 54.
(The winner to have exhibited in this show for at least 3 years, and not won a cup in the last 10 years)
JIMMY GRIFFITHS SHIELD & Blue Ribbon Award for the highest total points in the show.

SHOW AWARDS

COTTAGERS CUP for the best collection of vegetables in class 26.
WYNDHAM CUP for the best bowl of mixed flowers in class 48.
NICHOLSONS SILVER JUBILEE CUP for the best exhibit in the floral classes.
R. HAYDON CUP for the best exhibit in the Gladioli classes.
MILLENNIUM TROPHY & Red Ribbon Award for the best exhibit in the show.

Mr Withycombe of the Luttrell Arms Hotel and in the evening there was dancing.

The full history of the Horticultural Society is yet to be discovered. There were certainly shows in the first part of the twentieth century and a schedule for 1939 expects good entries. Karl Meddick recalls that the show that started on the Lawns was later moved to the grassy area in front of the castle. However, after a show was ruined by bad weather, the venue was changed to the Memorial Hall.

Over the last few years the show has suffered some disappointments but in 2001, entries exceeded all expectations.

Sam Hardwick, head gardener at Dunster Castle for many years. After his death in 1957 his second wife, Mollie, began her collection of 250 dolls that form the basis of Dunster's Doll Museum.

The Castle Gardens

In the 1920s and '30s at least seven gardeners were employed in the grounds of the castle and the complex of walled gardens under head gardener, Sam Hardwick, 'a most knowledgeable man'. R.J. Pearse, who worked there as a gardener from 1933, recalled how the gardens and shrubberies were well maintained and were home to rare shrubs and trees such as banana trees, *Lilium Giganteum, Dicksonia Antartica* (tree fern) and tropical bamboos planted in the mill walks and around the castle.

The gardens included a melon garden and two gardens in Mill Lane where there are now bungalows. Jim Copp came to work there in the early 1930s and was in charge of two vegetable gardens where he grew asparagus, celery, marrows and other vegetables. There were also various fruit trees including apples – Bramleys, Allison's Orange, Cox's Orange Pippin and Lord Lambourne – and quinces. Jim's daughter, June, remembers that young lads were employed to carry baskets of fruit and vegetables up to the castle. Geoffrey Rowe and Cyril Webber were two of them. During the Second World War Land Army girls – Margaret Parham, Ann Dunn and Alice Down – were employed to work in the castle gardens and nursery.

The Copp Family

Right: *Jim Copp and his family moved from Carhampton to Riverside Cottage in February 1940. One of the oldest cottages in Dunster, it had three bedrooms where Jim's wife Ethel later did bed and breakfast, welcoming guests from all over the world. When they moved in the cottage had running water but no electricity. Gas was laid on during the war but before that it was oil lamps, open fires and a range.*

Below: *The asparagus bed opposite Riverside, Park Street. Rose Cottage is in the background (c.1949–52).*

Above: *Jim Copp, c.1940.*

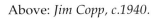

Prize-winning Veg

The Fish House stood in Mill Lane. By Jim Copp's day it was used for storing apples and having a quick break out of the rain. Unfortunately, this photograph has been damaged with the passage of time.

Below: *Jim all wrapped up in his work!*

Above: *Sowing seeds (c.1949–52).*

Prize-winning Veg

A prize marrow grown in the Fish House Garden (c.1949–52).

A fine crop of onions!

Transport by Horse

Horse-drawn vehicles were commonplace in Dunster in the 1920s. John Haydon recalled that John Vaulter from Aville Farm passed through the town daily with a cart laden with fruit and vegetables on its way to Minehead while Tom Winter, employed by the Hine brothers, builders, carried building material with heavy horse and wagon. Ted Giles delivered goods from the railway station and William Court – market gardener and furniture remover – was often seen with a wagon laden with household goods. The Dunster Castle estate timber wagons were drawn by three horses with Tom Huxtable driving and Bert Chubb as brakeman at the rear. Much skill and expertise was needed to negotiate the corner by Parham's shop. Another regular was James Gollop driving Mrs Wyndham in her pony carriage.

Right: *John Vaulter with vegetable supplies from Windwhistle, c.1934, before he moved to Aville. Behind the horse is John Hartnell outside his house in the High Street.*

Left: *A laden timber wagon negotiating the corner at the foot of the High Street.*

Right: *The timber wagon returning empty from Loxhole sawmills.*

Left: *Jim Gollop with his daughter Emmie and granddaughter Angela in Mrs Wyndham's trap.*

Allotments

There were allotments in Dunster by the 1920s; today they are managed by the Parish Council with many enthusiastic allotment-holders.

When Karl Meddick was courting in 1934 he was roundly reproved for wasting time with Violet, who was in service at the vicarage, instead of helping his father on the allotment. He has worked on the allotments ever since but his lapses were surely worth it for he has been happily married to Violet for 67 years.

Farming at Aville

Don Vaulter planting potatoes at Aville, c.1950.

John Vaulter in the 1920s mowing at Broadwood. After spells at Kitswall and Windwhistle, the Vaulters moved to Aville, c.1950.

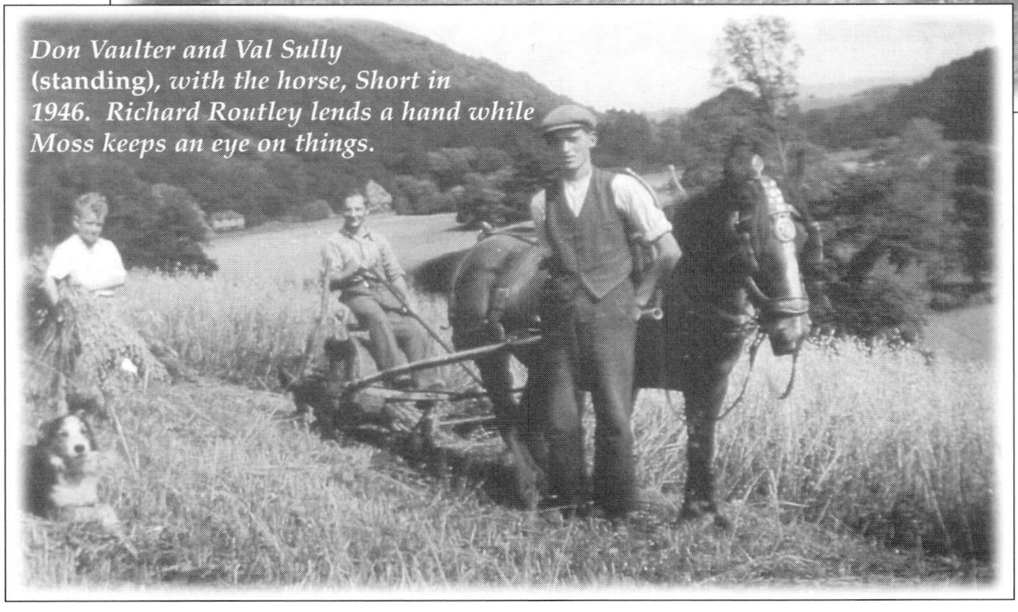

Don Vaulter and Val Sully **(standing)***, with the horse, Short in 1946. Richard Routley lends a hand while Moss keeps an eye on things.*

Farming at Aville

Aville, 1924, when Jack and Ethel Griffiths moved to the middle cottage, following their marriage.

Haymaking at Aville during the war. Joan Griffiths (now Vaulter) with Charlie Parminter.

Chapter Sixteen

SPECIAL EVENTS

One of several unidentified pictures that show military parades on Dunster Lawns, which are almost certainly linked to the Territorial Army camps held on North Hill in the 1890s and early 1900s.

Ye Elizabethan Fayre & Maske, 13 and 14 August 1931

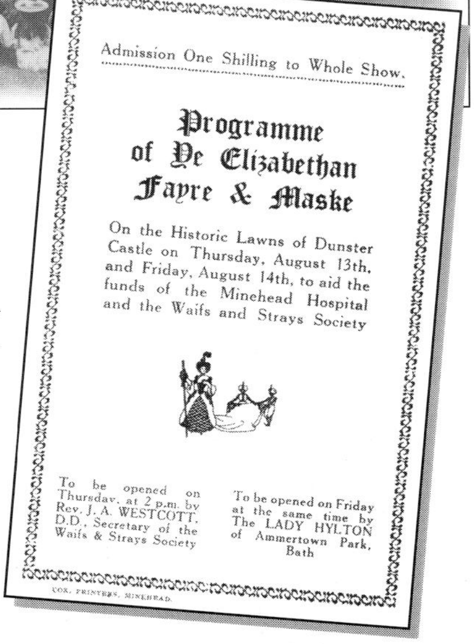

Admission One Shilling to Whole Show.

Programme of Ye Elizabethan Fayre & Maske

On the Historic Lawns of Dunster Castle on Thursday, August 13th, and Friday, August 14th, to aid the funds of the Minehead Hospital and the Waifs and Strays Society

To be opened on Thursday, at 2 p.m. by Rev. J. A. WESTCOTT, D.D., Secretary of the Waifs & Strays Society

To be opened on Friday at the same time by The LADY HYLTON of Ammertown Park, Bath

COX, PRINTERS, MINEHEAD.

This spectacular event in aid of the Minehead and West Somerset Hospital and the Waifs and Strays (now The Children's) Society was held to celebrate the fiftieth anniversary of the founding of the Society. Besides a memorable pageant, Dunster Lawns sported a realistic reconstruction of an Elizabethan village with 'shoppes' and refreshment stalls and the Yarn Market taking pride of place. There was also an Amusement Park with sideshows ranging from swingboats and coconut shies to a skittle alley and a hall of laughter. An orchestra under the direction of Captain W. Hook played selections of Elizabethan-style and patriotic music accompanied at the piano by Mrs Amherst.

Sir Walter Luttrell recalls that the pageant involved 'a large tented feudal village' – a much-magnified version of the Sealed Knot's encampment in Pond Meadow – and a two-day performance by some 50 or 60 costumed 'players', all recruited from local friends of the family:

Father was a very fine Henry VIII and Miss Acland-Hood from Fairfield was Anne Boleyn. I was a page and disgraced myself by having uncontrollable, and very obvious, giggles at their attempt to dance a stately pavane in rather long grass. I remember the impressive sight as some 20 caparisoned horses (several loaned by

Edgar Lamacraft) cantered 'on stage' from a screened assembly area. Unfortunately the 'halt' that had been successfully rehearsed with normal saddlery was not so successful on the opening day. Several riders found that flapping attachments to reins, stirrups and saddle-cloths completely neutralised any braking arrangements and, having scattered performers and spectators, the horses ended up down by the main road. Nevertheless it was all a tremendous spectacle, drew enormous crowds, and made a great deal of money for the charities.

Elizabethan Fayre

Left: *Some of the cast assembled on the steps of Dunster Castle.*

Right: *Queen Elizabeth was played by Mrs Robert Vernon who rode sidesaddle for the occasion.*

Left: *The Fayre. A lifesize model of the Yarn Market took centre stage.*

Elizabethan Fayre

Geoffrey Luttrell played Henry VIII while the Hon. Maud Acland-Hood took the part of Anne Boleyn.

1930s Celebrations

Left: *Dunster Castle was floodlit for the first time in 1935 in honour of the silver jubilee of King George V.*

West Street decorated for a royal event in the 1930s.

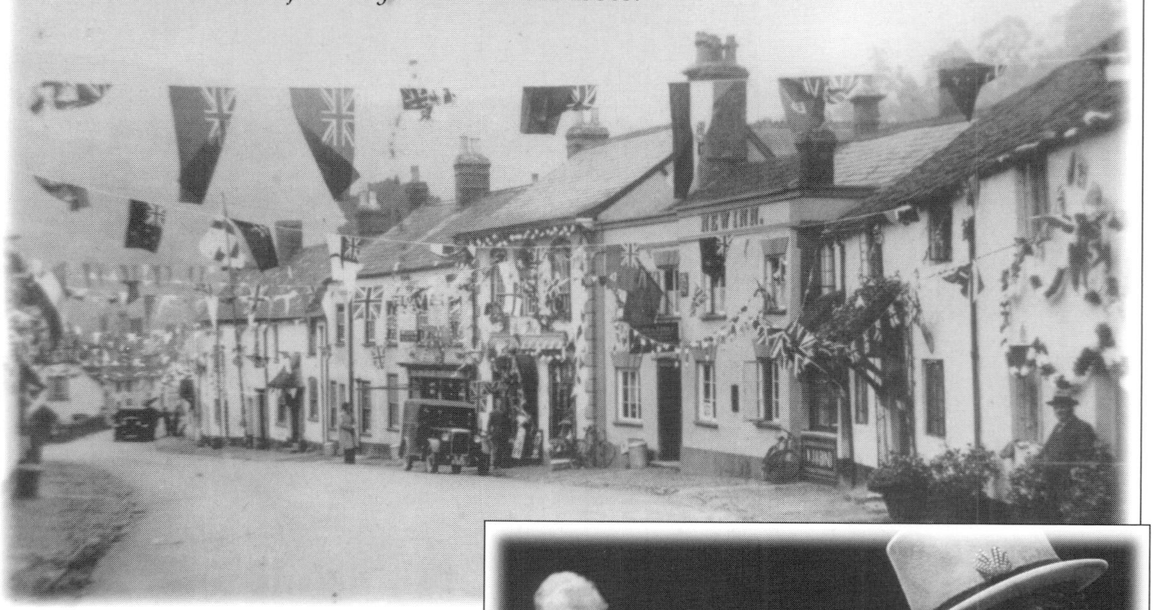

Right: *The Mickey Mouse travelling circus attracted many fascinated onlookers.*

VE Day

Dunster celebrated VE Day with a street party in the High Street. The Revd A.H. Balleine is to the left, below.

VE Day – Everyone Joined In

Above: *Mr Geoffrey Luttrell is seated on the extreme right.*

Festival of Britain

Dunster celebrated the Festival of Britain with a week of events that included a two-day Medieval Fair of such magnitude and splendour that it made the national press. J.B. Priestley wrote in *The Listener* (24 May 1951):

If I had to award a prize for terrific goings-on to a smallish place, my choice, I think, would be Dunster Parish, which from June 13 to 17 will have medieval booths, hucksters, jugglers, beggars, men in stocks, monks chanting round the church and priory gardens, minstrels, a band of recorders, three teams of archers, five morality plays, spinning and weaving, wool brought in on packhorses and spun on site, the hobby horse, morris and country dancing, exhibitions of local antiques and handicrafts, sports and teas for children, and a firework display. I call this prodigal. And somebody might write a film about such a village that went medieval for the Festival and then decided to stay in the Middle Ages.

Left: *The crowds were phenomenal.*

Right: *All the schoolchildren took part under the watchful eye of Mrs Davis.*

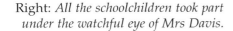

Left: *Maypole dancing on the Lawns.*

Festival of Britain

Below: *Weaving in the Yarn Market.*

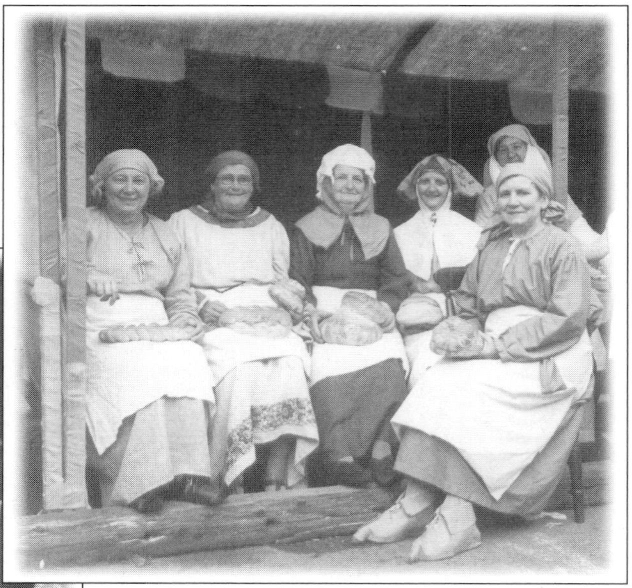

Above: *The baker's shoppe.*
Left to right: *Mrs Bob Upham, Mrs Bert Hole, Mrs Bowles, Mrs Charlie Griffiths, Mrs C. Tudball, Mrs George Maidment.*

One of the morality plays, **Dame Truth***, with Bill Dainton on the left.*

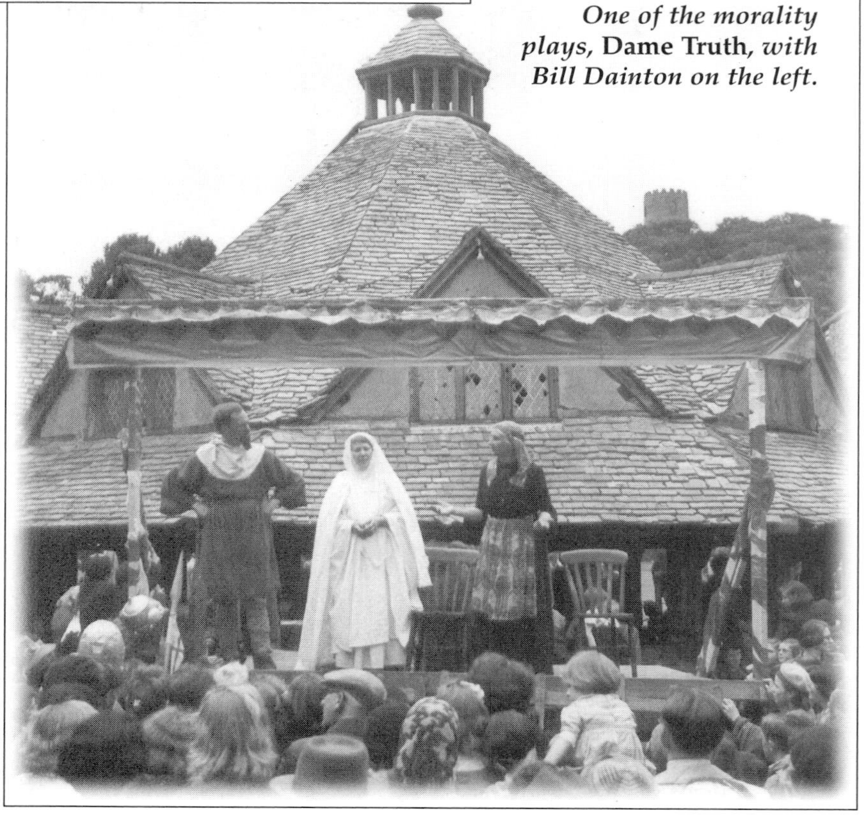

Festival of Britain

Above: Left to right, standing: *Harry Hallet, Jimmy Wilkinson, John Radford, Jack Tudball, Peter Tudball, Dennis Sully, George Maidment;* crouching: *A.N. Other.*

Above and left: *Schoolchildren at the celebrations. The lady in the black and white hat and dress was Mrs Pring, Dunster school teacher.*

The Coronation

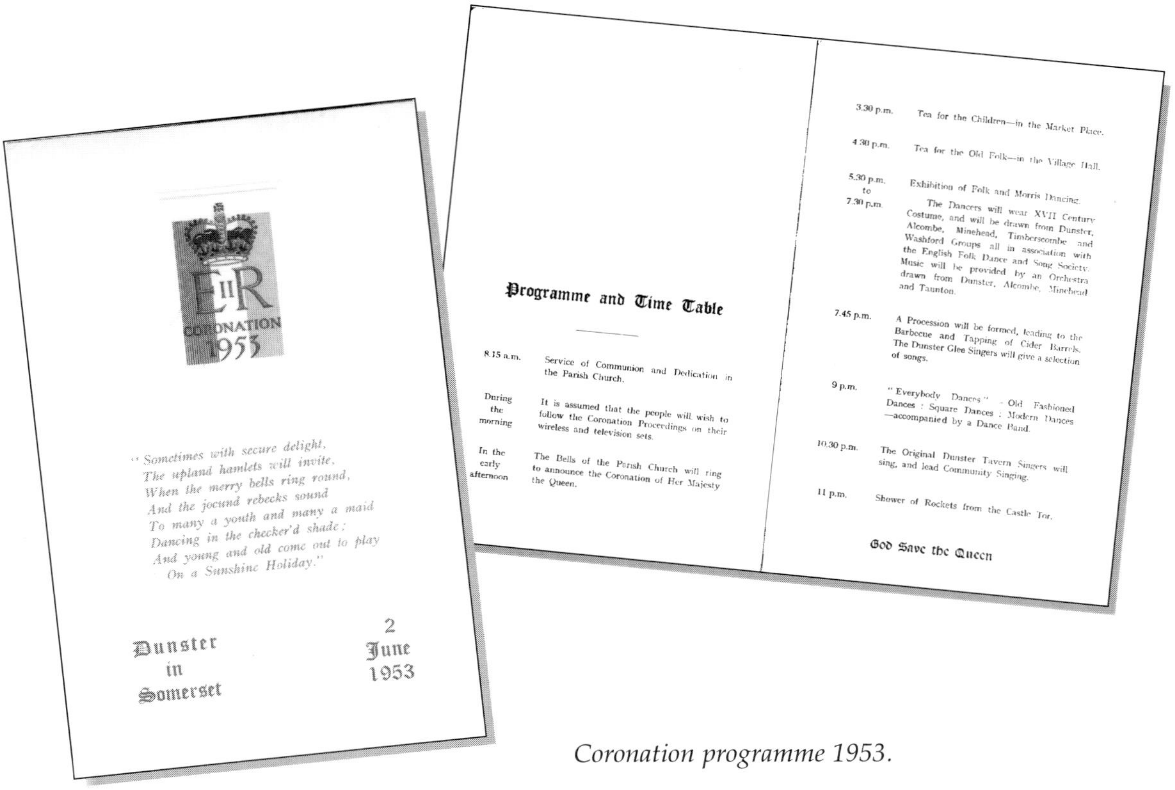

EIIR
CORONATION
1953

" Sometimes with secure delight,
The upland hamlets will invite,
When the merry bells ring round,
And the jocund rebecks sound
To many a youth and many a maid
Dancing in the checker'd shade;
And young and old come out to play
On a Sunshine Holiday."

Dunster in Somerset

2 June 1953

Programme and Time Table

8.15 a.m.	Service of Communion and Dedication in the Parish Church.
During the morning	It is assumed that the people will wish to follow the Coronation Proceedings on their wireless and television sets.
In the early afternoon	The Bells of the Parish Church will ring to announce the Coronation of Her Majesty the Queen.
3.30 p.m.	Tea for the Children—in the Market Place.
4.30 p.m.	Tea for the Old Folk—in the Village Hall.
5.30 p.m. to 7.30 p.m.	Exhibition of Folk and Morris Dancing. The Dancers will wear XVII Century Costume, and will be drawn from Dunster, Alcombe, Minehead, Timberscombe and Washford Groups all in association with the English Folk Dance and Song Society. Music will be provided by an Orchestra drawn from Dunster, Alcombe, Minehead and Taunton.
7.45 p.m.	A Procession will be formed, leading to the Barbecue and Tapping of Cider Barrels. The Dunster Glee Singers will give a selection of songs.
9 p.m.	" Everybody Dances " - Old Fashioned Dances : Square Dances : Modern Dances —accompanied by a Dance Band.
10.30 p.m.	The Original Dunster Tavern Singers will sing, and lead Community Singing.
11 p.m.	Shower of Rockets from the Castle Tor.

God Save the Queen

Coronation programme 1953.

Coronation decorations. Mr G. Foster won the prize for the best-decorated house.

Barbecue & Barrel

Below: *Deer roast in the old Deer Park.*

Below: *Tapping a barrel in the Yarn Market.*

Dunster folk are divided as to whether these pictures were taken at the Coronation or the Festival of Britain. However, a deer roast in the Old Park and the Tapping of cider barrels certainly took place at the Coronation.

Silver Jubilee Celebrations

The Ell family with friends outside Stagshead House, West Street.

The Revd Robert Doré and Arthur Ell.

Silver Jubilee Celebrations

Silver Jubilee Celebrations

One of the Munson brothers leads a dancing bear with Bob Thomas 'under the skin'.

Chapter Seventeen

SPORTS & ORGANISATIONS

The WI was always renowned for its teas – at the silver jubilee in 1978 for example, they provided a tea for 178 adults and 100 children. Here Miss Daisy Court, Mrs Webber, Miss Dolly Winter, Mrs Coles, Mrs Wyburn, Mrs Furse and Mrs Lovell do the honours.

The Women's Institute

At an inaugural meeting on 20 February 1920 held in the Parish Hall at 24/26 High Street, the decision was taken to form a Women's Institute in Dunster. Miss Mary Luttrell, who was one of the instigators, became the group's first president while Miss Constance Haughton, the daughter of the Methodist minister, became secretary.

The main aim of the newly-formed movement was to give country women the opportunity of working together to improve their quality of life in rural areas and to provide a variety of educational and leisure activities – something that could be of nothing but benefit to poorly educated country women. Until this time, only the girls who went into service in the big houses were taught the finer skills of household management.

Since its formation, there has been plenty of serious business and activity for the Women's Institute of Dunster; it has always been a lively group with competitions that in the early years included the 'Best darned sock' and 'A 2-course dinner for 2 for under a shilling'. For many years a motto was chosen annually to set the tone – in 1940 and 1942 it was:

Do Zummat,
Do good if you can,
But do Zummat.

Dunster WI held a regular market stall in the Yarn Market from 1921 until 1934 and throughout the war until at least 1947. Vegetables and fruit given by villagers were sold as well as canned fruit and jams (1s.3d. for 2lbs), preserved as part of a government scheme. All proceeds went to the Red Cross. By 1945 Dunster WI members had made 2,813lbs. of jam under the scheme, not to mention all the chutneys and preserved fruit.

The Rifle Club

Ladies' Rifle Team. Left to right, standing: *Molly Davis, Molly Parkman;* seated: *Eileen Woodbury, Louie Mogg (Sparkes), Eva Simpson.*

The Ladies' Team were a branch of the Dunster British Legion Rifle Club who met in the village at the Club Hut on the Green.

Sports Teams

At the end of the nineteenth century the cricket pitch and pavilion were situated near Henstey Wood. Later the pitch was moved to the other side of the main road and was situated in a field nearer the sea.

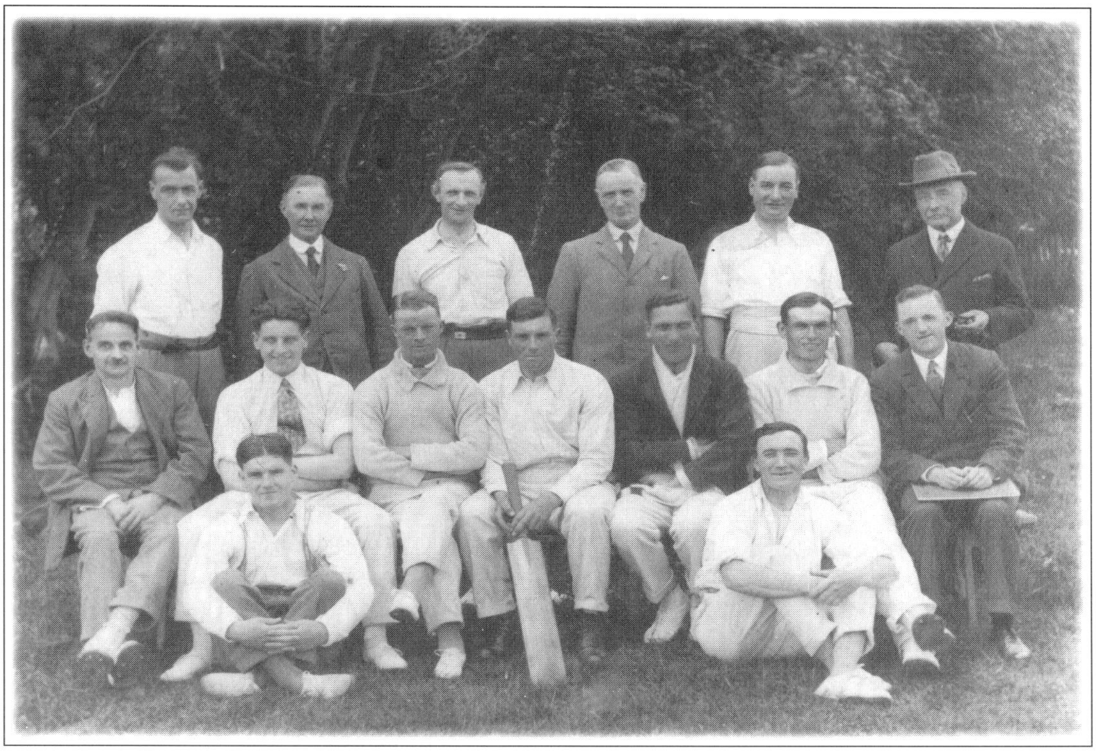

Dunster Cricket Club in the late 1920s. Left to right, back row: *W. Tudball, Mr Patfield, ? Tame, Mr Cuthill, J.J. Hole, ?;* centre: *?, ?, W. Webber, ?, W.J. Mackenzie, D. Burge, M. O'Shea;* front: *E. Hurford and Mr Bendle.*

Dunster Tug-of-War team, 1926.

Football

Left: *Dunster Association Football Team, 1907–8, winners of the Junior League.*

Right: *The footballers pictured include,* back row: *Bert Tapp, Ken Meddick* (third from left), *Gilbert Sparkes* (fifth from left); front: *Jack Haydon, Stan Miller, Tom Poole, Jack Parham and A.N. Other.*

Dunster Association Football Club, 1926–27. Winners of the W.S.J. Hospital Cup, W.S. Charity Cup, W.S. Knockout Cup, W.S.J. League Cup. (Photo by Alfred Vowles, Minehead)
Left to right, back row: *J.J. Hole, W.J.O. Bond, S. Burge, G.O. Bond, D.N. Williams, A.H.S. Baker, S. Ell (Hon. Secretary);* centre: *J. Parham, F. Case, J. Tudball (Captain), G. Sparks, A. Tudball;* front: *V. Tapp, S. Miller, W. Tudball, G. Cuthill, H. Perry.*

Dunster Girl Guides

Above: *Robin Patrol, 1945.* Left to right: *Marjorie Moggridge, June Copp, Suzanne Cole, Gwen Heywood and Jackie Udell.*

Above: *Margaret Gould, Robin Patrol, 1948.*

Left to right, back row: *Jean Bowden, Margaret Burge, Doris Winter;* front: *Enid Davey, Pam Gould, Audrey Wedlake.*

Dunster Guides & Scouts

Left: *Dunster Girl Guides, 1945 with Guider Miss Todd* (centre front). *Both the Guides and Scouts met in the Scout Hut that was situated on Dunster Steep beside the Luttrell Arms Garage. In 1962 it was moved to the Marsh to make way for the refurbished garage and became St George's Hut.*

Right: *Dunster Rover Scouts, c.1930.* Left to right, back row: *Bill Furse, Fred Yeandle, Miss Margaret Todd, Jack Haydon, Ernie Hurford;* front: *Jack Gould, Cecil Dibble, Jim Griffiths, Bill Mandley.*

Left: *Dunster Scouts. Does anybody look familiar?*

Right: Left to right, back row: *Archie Poole, ?, ?, ?, ?;* centre: *Bert Tapp, Ken Meddick;* front: *Jack Parham, Gilbert Sparkes, Jack Haydon, Jack Baker, Stan Mitter, Tom Poole?, Eric Yeandle.*

Dunster Bell-ringers

Above: *Maureen Tudball and Jean Bowden are instructed by J. Tudball* (left) *and A. Tudball at Dunster.*

Above: *Tom Elliot, veteran of the Dunster Band of Bell-ringers, 1948.*

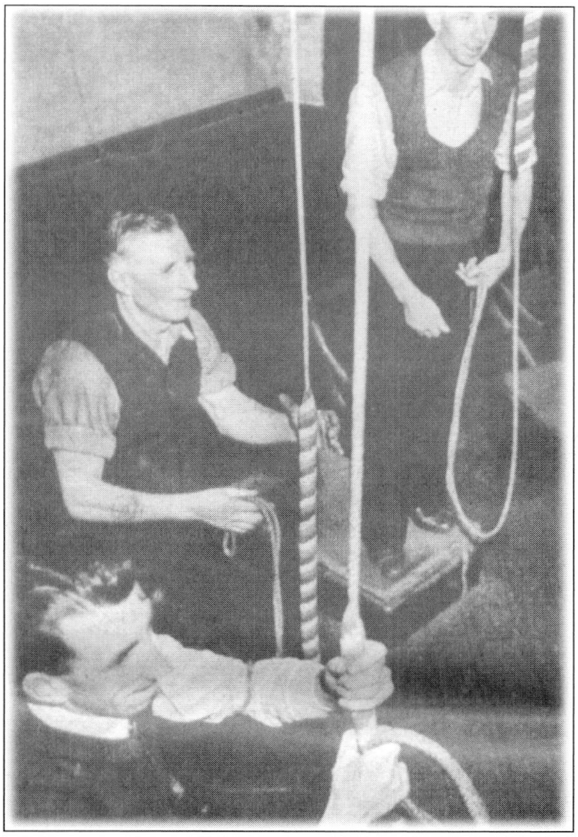

Left: *In Dunster Tower. Mr I. Farmer, the conductor, with Mr H. Lloyd and a visiting ringer* (in the foreground).

Bell-ringers' Outing, 1948

In 1948 the bell-ringers visited a number of towers in North Devon.

Left: *In Chittlehampton ringing chamber.* Left to right: *Mr J. Parker, Mr I. Farmer, Mr H. Lloyd, Revd Mr Cockle, Mr W. Tudball and Mr J. Herod.*

Right: *The bell-ringers sign the visitors' book in the ringing chamber at Okehampton.*

POSTSCRIPT: PRESENT & FUTURE

Haymaking at Dunster, 1912.

Left: *Dunster High Street, c.1895. Centre right is the building that originally housed the butchers' shambles with Dunster Reading Room upstairs. By 1895 the lower part of the building was used as a Parish Hall. On the right is the Lion Inn and beyond the saddlery. On the near left is the Horse and Crook Inn.*

The first decades of the twentieth century were, for many in Dunster, not easy times. While there was work available, especially in the building trade, wages were not high and many families found it hard to make ends meet. Often the womenfolk supplemented their husbands' wages by cleaning, taking in washing or running a small business. Jack Haydon, for example, remembers that when he was a lad his father was a carpenter on the Dunster Castle estate, while his mother worked very hard at various jobs. He also recalls being sent to the vicarage when the Revd F. Hancock was there for a jug of soup twice a week. He used to deliver groceries from Parham's to Lower Marsh on a pair of trucks.

It was the lack of good work prospects together with the inducements of the Canadian government that inspired six young lads from Dunster to leave for Canada in April 1913. Dunster Band accompanied them as they walked to the station, with mixed feelings of joy and regret, on the first leg of their journey. Some, like Edgar Dyer, were to return; others, like Bob Tudball, remained in Canada for the rest of their lives.

Alice Gould

Alice Gould, mother to Phyl Fennell of Old Cleeve. She married William Webber, son of John Webber, born at Clicket near Timberscombe.

Three Generations of Goulds

Above: *Elizabeth Gould (Lizzy), daughter of Granny Gould. She married Dick Wedlake from Watchet and was widowed during the First World War.*

Granny Gould c.1910 outside her cottage, the right-hand portion of which is now Cavill Cottage in St George's Street.

Left: *Lizzy with her daughter, Dolly, soon after her husband was killed.*

Right: *On the left is Sidney Court who lived with his sister, Daisy, at the back of Granny Gould's cottage. They were first cousins of the Goulds and after both Daisy and Granny Gould had died Sidney went to live with Lizzy and Dolly. They are pictured with Lizzy's grandchildren, Audrey and Shirley.*

The Griffiths

Inset: *Richard and Mary Farmer of West Street, the parents of Jane Griffiths.*

Mabel Griffiths (Bowden) with a young relative, c.1925. She was a pupil teacher at Dunster School.

Reginald and Jane Griffiths (née Farmer). Reginald was a stonemason on the Dunster Castle estate and Jane worked in the kitchen at the castle. She died of appendicitis in 1925. Her daughter, Mabel, then looked after her father and when she married Louis Bowden they continued to live in the house at the foot of Castle Hill.

Dunster Town Band. Front right is Wilfred, Wes Gould's father.

In 1951 he wrote from Winnipeg to the editor of the West Somerset Free Press:

When we arrived here we did not receive a royal welcome, but found the rivers still frozen, and lots of snow, and hundreds of persons unemployed, and jobs difficult to find. It was then we decided that everyone must start pioneering and look after himself, with the result that we were widely separated and lost contact with each other. When the first war broke out in 1914 it seems that some of the boys went overseas and did not return to this country.

Left: *John (Jack) Haydon was born in 1908 in Mill Lane to a poorish family living with their in-laws. George Elliott was a sort of odd-job man – town crier, haircutter, snob* [bootmaker] *and so on – he used to be landlord of the New Inn. The family also kept various tollgates in Somerset including that at Dunster. They had nine children of whom Caroline, Jack's mother, was the sixth, born in 1871. Granny Elliott was blind but could knit and sew nearly as well as those who could see.*

Bob did not return to England and died in Canada in the 1970s.

Several of the pictures in this book were scanned from a volume of photographs of Dunster published by Alfred Vowles in 1912. The volume, for sale on a stall in Winnipeg, caught the eye of Roberta Woods who had trained as a nurse with Jill White, now of Leighland. It seems likely that the book was sent out to one of the lads in Canada by a loving family in Dunster. It was in pristine condition so it is hard to know whether the book was preserved with especial care or whether it was simply put away, out of sight, an unnecessary reminder of times past.

During the first half of the twentieth century in spite of the two world wars, the growth of transport and a steady flow of 'curious visitors' the pace of change at Dunster was slow. The catalogue setting out details of the Dunster estates when they were sold in 1951 included a photograph of the High Street looking towards the Yarn Market. Trees are in full leaf, there are three parked cars, discreet signs advertising refreshments and postcards and not a person in sight. The properties for sale included long-established businesses, the smithy and the saddlery, builders and a coal merchants, butcher, tailor, grocer and chemist. With a newsagent, Post Office and visiting bank the town was still virtually self-sufficient.

Many of the existing tenants did buy their own properties in the 1951 sale although it was not always easy for them to raise the necessary capital.

Over the next 20 years or so, following the national trend, small shops and businesses were given up thus leaving the way clear for fresh faces to move into Dunster.

Today the essential Dunster still exists but the growth in leisure time and the current interest in things past have combined to turn the town into a tourist honeypot, and catering for the needs of the visitor makes economic sense. There are few businesses left that serve the needs of the town all the year round and many people have chosen to come to live in Dunster in order to run businesses concerned with the needs of the visitor. Nonetheless there is still a real community spirit in the town enhanced by the church and the school as well as by the many organisations such as the Parish Council, Dunster Village Society and the Women's Institute with their varied concerns for the well-being of this special place.

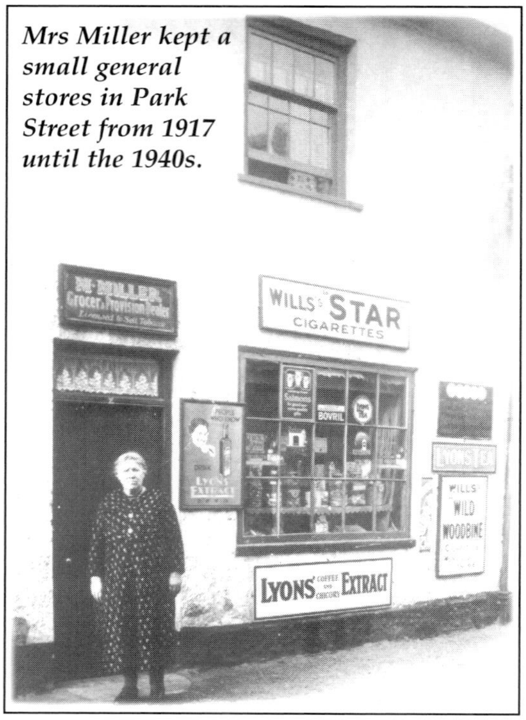

Mrs Miller kept a small general stores in Park Street from 1917 until the 1940s.

That Dunster lies within Exmoor National Park is to its advantage for the Park Authority is able to exercise a degree of control, which ensures that the town retains its character and does not turn itself into another Land's End. This is helped too by the presence of the National Trust at the castle and to a lesser extent by the Crown Commissioners who own and administer much of the wood and farmland surrounding the town.

If Dunster is to thrive in the twenty-first century and, at the same time, retain its unique character, everyone concerned with its future will need to work together to ensure that the visitors who maintain its economic viability neither damage nor obscure the essence of the place they have come to enjoy. I am sure that this will happen if Dunster continues to be a living community of people who love living in the town.

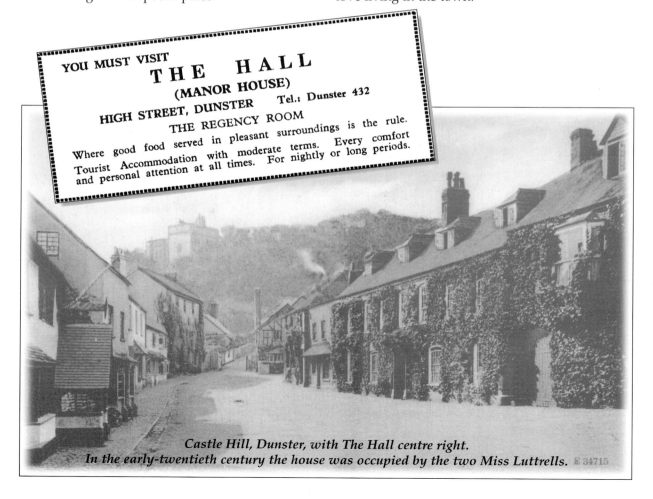

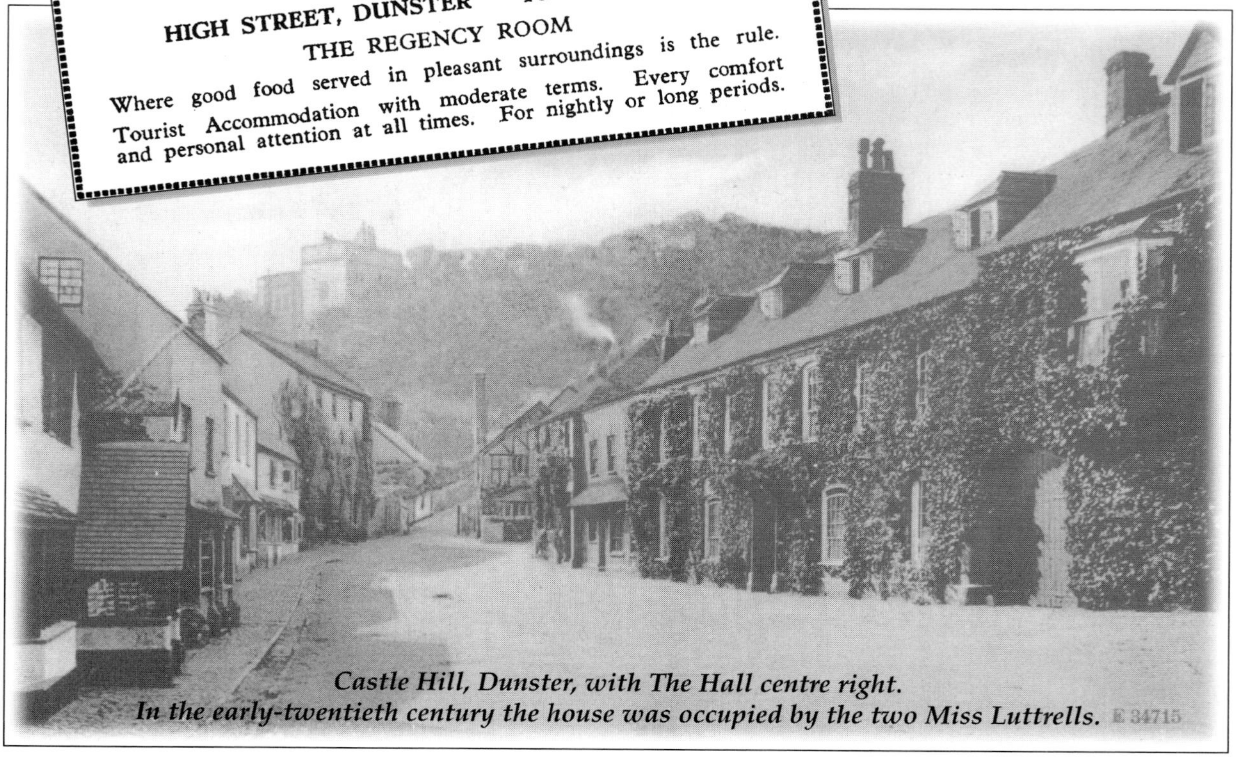

Castle Hill, Dunster, with The Hall centre right.
In the early-twentieth century the house was occupied by the two Miss Luttrells.

Garages

Pike's Garage in St George's Street built originally for Mr C. Ell in the 1930s. It was demolished in 1998 to make way for new housing.

PHONE: DUNSTER 237.

TELEPHONE:
DUNSTER
237.

FOR
PRIVATE
CAR HIRE.

TRAINS MET
TO
ORDER.

C. J. ELL.

THE GARAGE,
DUNSTER,
SOMERSET.

Luttrell Arms Garages

Left: *In the 1920s Louis Bowden was working for Hardy's Motors and often drove groups from Dunster to visit Gough's Caves in Cheddar. In 1929 he opened a garage in the town.*

Right: *One of the first Dunster taxis, an Austin 12 owned by Louis Bowden.*

Right: *The Luttrell Arms Garage in the early 1930s. Standing between Louis* (third right) *and Mabel Bowden is Cyril Sully.*

Left: *The petrol pumps, c.1937. Two elm trunks supported the shelter.*

Luttrell Arms Garage

The Land's End Trials, 1954. Centre left is Aubrey Haydon.

Right: *Land's End Trials, 1954. In the background can be seen Harry Eames' orchard, site of the memorial to an unknown horse* (see page 78) *and now the main car park. The Garage's cars used to be parked under the trees.*

Left: The refurbished garage, rebuilt during 1963 and ready for use in 1964.

New Cars for the Castle

Louis Bowden delivers new Humbers to Mr and Mrs Geoffrey Luttrell.

Dunster School

Dunster School, c.1932.
Left to right, back row: *Miss Chilcott, John Cockrem, Gordon Griffiths, Ken Radford, Jack Rowe, Nolan Phelps, Bill Greenslade, Miss Harris;* third row: *Eleanor O'Shea, Edie Jones, Della Miller, Betty Court, ?, ?, Florrie Taylor;* second row: *Joy Grant, Joan Griffiths, Leslie Farmer, Betty Griffiths, Violet Hartnell, Mary Hartnell, Phyllis Caddy, Barbara Gould;* front row: *(?)Jim Gould, ? Rowe, Denis Radford, Michael Case, Tony Williams, ? Webber.*

Dunster School, 1963, with Miss Forster (left) who later married Canon Swann. Headmaster Mr Powles is on the right.

School, 1967.

Traffic through Dunster

Right: *Coming down Dunster Steep too fast one lunchtime in 1938, this Blue Motors bus landed up near where Riverside is today!*

Above: *Buses through Dunster, c.1960s. Traffic lights have since been installed to control the flow of vehicles through the narrow main street.*

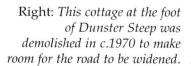

Right: *This cottage at the foot of Dunster Steep was demolished in c.1970 to make room for the road to be widened.*

Dunster Memorials

The Memorial Hall (the white building on the right of the picture) *was opened in 1923 in a refurbished malthouse and store, in memory of the men of Dunster who fell in the First World War.*

The Memorial Garden in the right foreground was given to the parish in perpetuity in 1953 by Geoffrey and Alys Luttrell.

Mason at Work

Roy Sparkes, monumental mason.

SUBSCRIBERS

Mike Arnold, Alcombe, Minehead, Somerset
Nigel Austen, Tonbridge, Kent
Tim Austen, East Malling, Kent
Alan Austen, East Malling, Kent
Alan and Lynda Baker, Alcombe, Somerset
Pauline and David Batten, Carhampton, Somerset
Ned, Katy, George and Joseph Binding, Taunton, Somerset
Steve and Jackie Bowden
Jane and Terry Brady, Nashville, USA
Mercia and Jim Brown, Saffron Walden
K.J. Burrow, Bucks Cross, Devon
Janet and Mike Capel, Dunster, Somerset
Peter and Aine Carter, Bossington Lane, Porlock, Somerset
John and Chris Carter, Astbury, Cheshire
Valerie Chidgey, Minehead, Somerset
Florence Clark, Highbridge, Somerset
Charles 'John' Cockrem, Minehead, Somerset
June Copp, Minehead, Somerset
Mrs M. Coveney, Welford-on-Avon, Warwickshire
Sheila and Philip Cross, Dunster, Somerset
Colin J. Curling and Patricia N. Grocock, Alcombe, Minehead, Somerset
Major John Alexander Cuthill, Perranporth, Cornwall
C.L. Degg ATCL, LTCL, Sneyd Green, Stoke-on-Trent, Staffordshire
Ken Dibble, Rugby, Warwickshire
Nolan A. Dibble, Rugby, Warwickshire
Mr K. Dixon, Hyde, Manchester
Toni and Ray Drew, East Twickenham, Middlesex
Douglas Dyer, Oldland Common, Bristol
Lorna M. Dyson, Bridgwater, Somerset
Gladys Earnshaw, Glemsford, Suffolk
D. Eldridge, Briddicott, Guildford, Surrey
C. and A. Ell, Dunster, Somerset
Ann P.P. Feldberg, Minehead, Somerset
Phyllis J. Fennell (née Webber), Old Cleeve, Somerset
M. June Francis, Carhampton, Somerset
Margaret Gould, Dunster, Somerset
Gordon I. Griffiths, Dunster, Somerset
Derek I. Griffiths, Dunster, Somerset
Kathleen Haste, Taunton
Jonathan M. Hawes, Enfield
Mrs M.A. Hawkins, Minehead, Somerset
Robin and Maureen Hawkins, Alcombe, Somerset
Wendy E. Hayes, Fareham, Hampshire
Margaret Heath, Alcombe, Somerset
Wg Cdr and Mrs R.B.G. Hedgecock
Jean Hodge (née Bowden), Dunster, Somerset
Julie A. Hole (née Slader), Dunster, Somerset
Mr Anthony J. Knight, Ellicombe, Minehead
Michael Leat, Bristol
Colin and Judith Lill, Northampton
Avril Liversidge, Knowle, Dunster, Somerset
Noel C. Lock, Dunster, Somerset
Adrian J. Locke, Tottenham, London
Julian C. Locke, Tottenham, London
Carole P. Mackereth, Dulverton, Somerset
Catherine and Alan Martin, Wiveliscombe, Somerset
Derrick J. Matthews, born Minehead, Somerset
John and Louise Melbourne, Dunster, Somerset
V.J. Miles, Minehead, Somerset
Mrs Molly E. Moore, Minehead, Somerset
Denise Nobbs, Watchet, Somerset
Hilda Parham, Dunster, Somerset

Mr John Parham, Taunton, Somerset
Mr Jim Parham, Dunster, Somerset
Sylvia Parsons (née Sully), Dunster, Somerset
Helen M. Pausey, Alcombe, Somerset
John, Janina, John, Edward and Robert (decd 7/02) Peach, formerly of Dunster
Muriel Petford, Malvern, Worcestershire
Nigel and Sue Pike, Bilbrook, Somerset
Rachel M. Pope, Carhampton, Somerset
Dr Guy and Dr Jenny Baverstock Poppy, Romsey, Hampshire
V.C. Poppy, Carhampton, Somerset
John and Shirley Potter, Dunster, Somerset
Jane and Mike Pretty, Minehead, Somerset
Clive Price, Minehead, Somerset
Gerald Price, Alcombe, Somerset
Gary Price, Timberscombe, Somerset
Edna Pritchard, Minehead, Somerset
Michael J. Rowe
Ken Runnels-Moss, Minehead, Somerset
Malcolm Scott, Minehead, Somerset
M. and H. Sekulla, Pinocchio Toys, Dunster, Somerset
Lesley Sharp, Carhampton, Somerset
C.P. Sharp OBE, Maulden, Bedfordshire
Yvonne Shaw, Dunster, Somerset
Mrs W.M. Shuttleworth
B. and J. Skudder, Doniford, Somerset
Mandy J. Stevens, Carhampton, Somerset
Tric and Gareth Storey
Robert M. Taylor, Minehead, Somerset
Patricia and Stan Taylor, Bristol
Chris and Rosalind Tigwell, Rainhill
Susan A. Townsend, Yarde Down, South Molton, Devon
Peter and Margaret Tudball
Joan Vaulter, Dunster, Somerset
A. Walford (née Giles), Minehead, Somerset
Susan and Keith Walley, Staffordshire
John F.W. Walling, Newton Abbot, Devon
Philip Webber, Dunster, Somerset
Russell Welsh, Dunster, Somerset
Andy Welsh, Dunster, Somerset
The Welsh family, Dunster (1896)
E.M. Williams, Alcombe, Minehead, Somerset
J. Wimblett and C. Elmer, Dunster, Somerset
S. and I.M. Witherford, Dunster, Somerset

Titles from the Series

The Book of Addiscombe • Various
The Book of Addiscombe, Vol. II • Various
The Book of Bampton • Caroline Seward
The Book of Barnstaple • Avril Stone
Book of Bickington • Stuart Hands
Blandford Forum: A Millennium Portrait • Various
The Book of Bridestowe • R. Cann
The Book of Brixham • Frank Pearce
The Book of Buckland Monachorum & Yelverton • Hemery
The Book of Carshalton • Stella Wilks
The Parish Book of Cerne Abbas • Vale & Vale
The Book of Chagford • Ian Rice
The Book of Chittlehamholt with Warkleigh & Satterleigh • Richard Lethbridge
The Book of Chittlehampton • Various
The Book of Colney Heath • Bryan Lilley
The Book of Constantine • Moore & Trethowan
The Book of Cornwood & Lutton • Various
The Book of Creech St Michael • June Small
The Book of Cullompton • Various
The Book of Dawlish • Frank Pearce
The Book of Dulverton, Brushford, Bury & Exebridge • Various
The Book of Dunster • Hilary Binding
The Ellacombe Book • Sydney R. Langmead
The Book of Exmouth • W.H. Pascoe
The Book of Grampound with Creed • Bane & Oliver
The Book of Hayling Island & Langstone • Rogers
The Book of Helston • Jenkin with Carter
The Book of Hemyock • Clist & Dracott
The Book of Hethersett • Various
The Book of High Bickington • Avril Stone
The Book of Ilsington • Dick Wills
The Book of Lamerton • Ann Cole & Friends
Lanner, A Cornish Mining Parish • Scharron Schwartz & Roger Parker
The Book of Leigh & Bransford • Various
The Book of Litcham with Lexham & Mileham • Various
The Book of Loddiswell • Various
The Book of Lulworth • Rodney Legg
The Book of Lustleigh • Joe Crowdy
The Book of Manaton • Various
The Book of Markyate • Richard Hogg
The Book of Mawnan • Various
The Book of Meavy • Pauline Hemery
The Book of Minehead with Alcombe • Binding & Stevens
The Book of Morchard Bishop • Jeff Kingaby
The Book of Newdigate • John Callcut
The Book of Northlew with Ashbury • Various
The Book of North Newton • Robins & Robins
The Book of North Tawton • Various
The Book of Okehampton • Radford & Radford
The Book of Paignton • Frank Pearce
The Book of Penge, Anerley & Crystal Palace • Various
The Book of Peter Tavy with Cudlipptown• Various
The Book of Pimperne • Jean Coull
The Book of Plymtree • Tony Eames
The Book of Porlock • Denis Corner
Postbridge – The Heart of Dartmoor • Reg Bellamy
The Book of Priddy • Various
The Book of Rattery • Various
The Book of Silverton • Various
The Book of South Molton • Various
The Book of South Stoke • Various
South Tawton & South Zeal with Sticklepath • Radfords
The Book of Sparkwell with Hemerdon & Lee Mill • Pam James
The Book of Staverton • Pete Lavis
The Book of Stithians • Various
The Book of Studland • Rodney Legg
The Book of Swanage • Rodney Legg
The Book of Torbay • Frank Pearce
Uncle Tom Cobley & All: Widecombe-in-the-Moor • Stephen Woods
The Book of Watchet • Compiled by David Banks
The Book of West Huntspill • Various
Widecombe-in-the-Moor • Stephen Woods
The Book of Williton • Michael Williams
Woodbury: The Twentieth Century Revisited • Roger Stokes
The Book of Woolmer Green • Various

Forthcoming

The Book of Bakewell • Various
The Book of Barnstaple, Vol. II • Avril Stone
The Book of Brampford • Various
The Book of Breage & Gurmoe • Stephen Polglase
The Book of the Bedwyns • Various
The Book of Bideford • Peter Christie
The Book of Bridport • Rodney Legg
The Book of Buckfastleigh • Sandra Coleman
The Book of Carharrack • Various
The Book of Castleton • Geoff Hill
The Book of Edale • Gordon Miller
The Book of Kingskerswell • Various
The Book of Lostwithiel • Barbara Frasier
The Book of Lydford • Barbara Weeks
The Book of Lyme Regis • Rodney Legg
The Book of Nether Stowey • Various
The Book of Nynehead • Various
The Book of Princetown • Dr Gardner-Thorpe
The Book of St Day • Various
The Book of Sampford Courtenay with Honeychurch • Stephanie Pouya
The Book of Sculthorpe • Garry Windeler
The Book of Sherborne • Rodney Legg
The Book of Southbourne • Rodney Legg
The Book of Tavistock • Gerry Woodcock
The Book of Thorley • Various
The Book of Tiverton • Mike Sampson
The Book of West Lavington • Various
The Book of Witheridge • Various
The Book of Withycombe • Chris Boyles

For details of any of the above titles or if you are interested in writing your own history, please contact: Commissioning Editor Community Histories, Halsgrove House, Lower Moor Way, Tiverton Business Park, Tiverton, Devon EX16 6SS, England; email: naomic@halsgrove.com

In order to include as many historic photographs as possible in this volume, a printed index is not included. However, the Community History Series is indexed by Genuki. For further information and indexes to volumes in the series, please visit: http://www.cs.ncl.uk/genuki/DEV/indexingproject.html